William J Fay 3

TEXT AND INTERPRETATION

ECCLESIASTES

A Practical Commentary

J. A. Loader

Translated by John Vriend

GRAND RAPIDS, MICHIGAN
WILLIAM B. EERDMANS PUBLISHING COMPANY

Translated from the Dutch edition *Prediker: Een praktische bijbelverklaring*,
part of the Tekst en Toelichting series. © Uitgeversmaatschappij J. H. Kok—
Kampen, 1984.

Library of Congress Cataloging in Publication Data

Loader, J. A., 1945–
 Ecclesiastes.

 (Text and interpretation)
 Translation of: Prediker.
 1. Bible. O.T. Ecclesiastes—Commentaries. I. Title. II. Series.
BS1475.3.L6313   1986   223'.8077   86-4266

ISBN 0-8028-0102-1

CONTENTS

CONTENTS

TRANSLATOR'S PREFACE

In translating this volume from the Dutch original, I have
consistently tried to make it both readable and readily useful,
for the pastor as well as for the layperson.

Bible quotations are from the Revised Standard Version,
except where the author's own translation was closer in letter
and spirit to another version. In those cases, I followed the
appropriate version—New International, New English, or occasionally other versions—and indicated this in the text. When
for some reason the translation was not intelligible without
additional explanation, I have supplied a footnote.

It is my earnest wish that users of this commentary may
derive as much pleasure and instruction from reading it as I
did in translating it.

—JOHN VRIEND

INTRODUCTION

I. THE NAME OF THE BOOK AND ITS PLACE
IN THE CANON

The book is known in the English-speaking world as Ecclesiastes, a title that comes to us from the Septuagint, the Greek translation of the Old Testament. The phenomenon of book titles, so familiar to us, was unknown when the Old Testament was written. At that time there was a practice, however, of adding at the beginning of books editorial headings that reflect later editorial opinion concerning the nature and authorship of the book Examples are Proverbs 1:1; Song of Solomon 1:1; and Ecclesiastes 1:1. At the beginning of the latter book we read the heading: "The words of the Preacher, the son of David, king in Jerusalem."

The word translated as "Ecclesiastes" or "the Preacher" (Heb. *Qoheleth*) occurs several times in the body of the book (1:1, 2, 12; 7:27; 12:8, 9, 10), but it occurs nowhere else in the Old Testament. The word originally denoted an office of ministry, and as a result it sometimes occurs with the definite article (7:27 and 12:8—*the* Preacher), but in most cases it appears simply as a proper name, Ecclesiastes. The meaning of the designation is not entirely certain, but it does relate to someone's official action in connection with an assembly— "someone who convenes or addresses an assembly" or "the Assembler." There is really no one term that fully encompasses and describes the role of the person referred to by *Qoheleth*, but in the commentary below we will follow the example of the RSV and call him "the Preacher."

The reader will find Ecclesiastes in a different location in different canons. In both Roman Catholic and Protestant Bibles the book is placed in the third division of the four-part canon, namely, the poetic-didactic division. In the Hebrew Bible, which has only three divisions, Ecclesiastes occurs in the last part, known as "the Writings." A subdivision of the Writings

1

comprises a collection of five books that were set aside after the sixth century A.D. to be read in synagogues at the time of the Jewish festivals. One of these books is Ecclesiastes, which was the prescribed reading during the Feast of Tabernacles. It is not exactly clear why this linkage was established, but the occasion for it may be found in the admonition of the Preacher to be always joyful and celebrative (9:7-9). After the twelfth century Ecclesiastes appears fourth among the five scrolls in most manuscripts because the Feast of Tabernacles was the fourth festival on the synagogal calendar.

The book's canonicity was not initially called into question. Fragments of the book have been found in the fourth cave of Qumran, the residence of the desert community of the Dead Sea. Since this find dates from approximately the second century B.C., we know that Ecclesiastes bore a certain canonical authority already in early times. That was also the case toward the end of the first century A.D., for the rabbis of the so-called Synod of Jamnia (Jabneh, about 20 kilometers south of present-day Jaffa), who were meeting at that time, did not remove the book from the list of holy Scriptures. Nevertheless, the canonical value of Ecclesiastes was questioned later by various rabbis. We know from the Mishna that some rabbis were of the opinion that the book did not "soil the hands," that is, that it was not canonical. From another Jewish writing, the Tosephta, we know that the inspiration of the book was called into question, and on that basis also its canonicity. The Talmud, in which extensive commentaries on the Mishna were collected, also reports the objection. Mentioned here also is the fact that some rabbis took offense at the discrepancy between Ecclesiastes and the rest of the Hebrew Bible (e.g., that between the rhetorical question, What does man gain by all the toil at which he toils? [1:3] and the rabbinical view that the observance of the entire law of Moses was indeed meaningful toil). Some also balked at the supposed inner contradiction in the book (e.g., that between 2:2, where laughter and pleasure are called senseless, and 8:15, where laughter and hence also pleasure are praised). The call to enjoy life in 11:9 ("walk in the ways of your heart and the sight of your eyes") was viewed as a contradiction of Numbers 15:39 ("[do] not . . . follow after your own heart and your own eyes"). The reference to a dead lion in 9:4 has even been taken as an insult to David. Generally speaking, it was the disciples of the rabbi

2

Shammai who questioned the canonical value of Ecclesiastes while the disciples of Hillel held the opposing view. Most of the objections date from the middle of the second century A.D. and later times but never found enough support to undermine the canonical status of the book. Such critical opinions concerning the canonicity of Ecclesiastes never occurred in the early Christian church, which always accepted it as holy Scripture.

II. AUTHORSHIP AND DATE

Solomon was traditionally considered the author of the book. This is understandable, for the superscription expressly says that the Preacher whose words are recorded in the book is "the son of David, king in Jerusalem." There is much evidence, however, that indicates that Solomon cannot possibly be the author.

In the first place, it is clear from the language of the book that any date prior to the fifth century B.C. is out of the question, whereas Solomon lived in the tenth century B.C. The Hebrew of the author shows considerable Aramaic influence, which is typical of the most recent of the books of the Old Testament. In addition, this Hebrew contains several Persian loan-words that could not have been used prior to the fifth century B.C. On the other hand, the book could not have been written later than about 180 B.C. It is about this time that the book of Sirach's grandson was completed, and this employs expressions and ideas borrowed from Ecclesiastes. Further, we have available data enabling us to bring these outer time limits closer together. The Hebrew is later than that of fifth century Ezra, Nehemiah, and Malachi; this indicates that the book cannot have originated before the fourth century. On the other hand, the book precedes the religious activism that arose in Palestine in the second century, and a book whose teaching runs so counter to that activism must already have gained considerable status over time to have been able to survive the spirit of that age. Similarly, the book must have existed for some years to have been held to be a holy book (during the first half of the second century) in Qumran. So, then, we arrive at the middle of the third century B.C. as the most probable time of origin—seven centuries after Solomon.

This conclusion implies that an explanation other than

the traditional must be given to the superscription. In 1:12–2:11 the Preacher introduces himself as Solomon (compare 1:13-17 with 1 Kings 4:29ff.; 2:7-10 with 1 Kings 4:21-28; 2:4-7 with 1 Chron. 27:27-31—the crown property of Solomon's father; 2:7 with 1 Chron. 10:5; 2:8 with 1 Chron. 25 and 2 Chron. 5:12-13). But in other parts of the book the author presents himself as a royal subject and not as king (for instance, in the words about injustice and corruption in the land in 3:16; 4:1; 5:7ff.; and 10:4ff.—words that would be unintelligible in the mouth of a king). The so-called royal fiction is a phenomenon we know from Egyptian wisdom literature. In it, too, there are instances that put the teachings of wisdom into the mouth of an earlier king. Since Solomon was known as the sage par excellence it is not hard to understand why the author (1:12–2:11) and the editor (1:1), following Egyptian usage, put the wisdom of an unknown teacher of the third century B.C. into the mouth of the great king who lived in the tenth century B.C. Although this was a literary convention, we can be grateful that later generations took the ascription to Solomon literally, for his authority undoubtedly contributed to the preservation of this precious book in the canon.

III. LITERARY GENRE

The Jewish editors who prepared the text of the Old Testament received the book not as poetry but as prose, as we can tell from the accent marks they added to the vowels, using a system that differs from the one they applied to poetic books. The Greek translators of the Old Testament, however, listed Ecclesiastes among the poetic books and so indicated that they held a different opinion. Literary analysis has shown that the Greek translators of the book were correct: in Ecclesiastes we are indeed dealing with poetry, but it is poetry that displays an unusual metrical pattern and an even more unusual form. This is by no means surprising for an unusual form is appropriate for unusual contents.

These poems belong to the category of wisdom literature, of which there are several representatives in the Old Testament, for instance, Proverbs and Job. Wisdom is concerned with the correct ordering of life. Wise action is that which integrates people harmoniously into the order God has created. The rules of life that prescribe how human beings must integrate themselves into that order are the precepts of wisdom, as we find them especially in Proverbs 10–29. But wisdom literature includes not only such short proverbs but also long didactic poems concerning problems from the sphere of wisdom (like Job) and collections of poems that critically examine the typical teachings of wisdom (like Ecclesiastes).

We are not adequately equipped, however, to appreciate the impact of the poems of Ecclesiastes with only this minimal knowledge of the general literary genre of the book. Every poem in the book is a reflection on one of the aspects of the central theme of the book. Such a meditation or reflection regularly employs a variety of typical forms of expression belonging to wisdom literature in general. A reflection may contain, for example, an admonition, a proverb, or a comparison. Since these short utterances are characteristic for wisdom literature in general they are also called genres. So there are more inclusive genres that contain ever smaller genres (wisdom literature → reflection → proverb → simile or comparison). Ecclesiastes uses these literary forms in such a pointed and special way that the reader of the book requires an overview of these conventions. We shall offer a few examples.

a. A *true saying* is the formulation of a generally applicable truth: "All is vanity and a striving after wind" (1:14). "There are righteous men to whom it happens according to the deeds of the wicked, and there are wicked men to whom it happens according to the deeds of the righteous" (8:14). Closely related to the true saying is the *proverb*, in which the experience of the order of life is expressed: "A threefold cord is not quickly broken" (4:12). "A living dog is better than a dead lion" (9:4). One can turn to almost any page in the book of Proverbs and find this kind of wisdom saying. They also occur in abundance in Mesopotamian collections.

b. The *"better than" saying* or comparative saying is a comparison between two things in which the priority of one over the other is stated. "Two are better than one, because they have a good reward for their toil" (4:9). A large number of these comparative sayings can be found in this book (see the first verses of chap. 7) as in wisdom literature in general (cf. Prov. 3:14; 8:11; 15:16-17; 16:8; 19:1; etc.).

c. The *"as . . . so" comparison* is of a different nature and occurs several times. "As you do not know how the spirit comes to the bones in the womb of a woman with child, so you do not know the work of God who makes everything" (11:5). See Proverbs 4:18-19; Job 21:18; and the wisdom psalm Psalm 127:4 for other such similes.

d. The *metaphor* is a forceful comparison in which image and reality (without comparatives) are equated. There is a good example in 7:26, where the woman *is* a snare, her heart *is* a trap, and her hands *are* chains (NIV). Compare Proverbs 5:19 where the wife *is* a lovely hind, a graceful doe.

e. A more extended genre in wisdom literature is the *parable*, a story intended to teach. The Preacher uses such short stories in 4:13-16 and 9:14-15 to express his conviction that wisdom is useless. A similar story occurs in Proverbs 7:6-23, which concerns the danger of the unchaste woman. A variant of such a teaching story, the fable, occurs often in Babylonian wisdom literature.

f. An *allegory* is a series of related metaphors, an example of which is 12:3-4 (also v. 6), which can be compared with Proverbs 5:15ff. A series of metaphors is used to describe old age in the first case and youthful marriage partners in the second.

g. A characteristic genre in Ecclesiastes is that of the *observation*, the report of what the Preacher has seen in life: "And I saw that all labor and all achievement spring from man's envy of his neighbor. This too is meaningless, a chasing after the wind" (4:4, NIV). It is typical for the wisdom teacher to formulate his observations (e.g., Prov. 7:6ff.; 24:30ff.; and in the wisdom psalm, Ps. 37:25, 35-36), and in Ecclesiastes these observations occur dozens of times. It gives an impression of an intense kind of observation, reflection, and conclusion.

h. Sometimes one finds in Ecclesiastes samples of *autobiographical narrative:* "I thought in my heart, 'God will bring to judgment both the righteous and the wicked, for there will be a time for every activity, a time for every deed' " (3:17, NIV). Other examples from wisdom literature are Job 7:4; 9:27; 32:7.

i. The *woe-cry* and the *beatitude* occur side by side: "Woe to you, O land, whose king is a child who does not know enough to consult a counselor and whose princes feast in the morning. Blessed are you, O land, whose king is of noble birth and whose princes eat at a proper time and not as drun-

6

kards!" (10:15b-17).* The beatitude is well known from its use in wisdom literature: Proverbs 3:13; 8:32; 14:21; 16:20; 20:7; Wisdom of Sirach 14:1-2; 25:8-9; and elsewhere.

j. The *antilogion* is a particularly interesting genre, because it contains an apparent contradiction between two opposites. An example occurs in Ecclesiastes 7:16-17 ("Do not be overrighteous . . . do not be overwicked"; "neither be overwise . . . and do not be a fool" [NIV]). The same phenomenon occurs in Proverbs 26:4 and 5 ("Answer not a fool" and "Answer a fool") and in certain Sumerian proverbs.

k. The *rhetorical question* is a question that presupposes its own answer. Ecclesiastes frequently uses this forceful form of speech (the expected answer is always negative) and so shows the same kind of preference that Job did (cf. Job 38 and 39): "The word of the king is supreme, and who may say to him, 'What are you doing?' " (8:4).

l. The Preacher, like the author of Proverbs, often uses the form of an *admonition.* It is used when a command is given or advice is offered, accompanied—which is the rule in Ecclesiastes—by a statement of motivation: "Be not quick to anger, for anger lodges in the bosom of fools" (7:9).

It is evident, therefore, that the Preacher both knows and uses the typical forms and conventions of wisdom literature. It is by these devices that he lets himself be known as a wisdom teacher who stands squarely in the tradition of ancient eastern wisdom.

IV. THE COMPOSITION

For years there have been two completely opposite views concerning the composition of Ecclesiastes. Some commentators are of the opinion that the book was composed systematically as a development of a theme; others think the book consists simply of a number of separate pieces. Attempts have even been made to point out different sources in the book. If any one thing is certain, however, it is that the style of the author is so consistently uniform, and the basic theme so consistently pursued, that there can be no question of different sources. But there are also so many repetitions in the book that we

*For an explanation of the author's translation of these verses, see the commentary on 10:15b-20.

cannot speak of a continuous development of its theme either. What appears to be left as the one remaining possibility is the view that the book consists of a loose collection of separate utterances. But even that is not the case. The poems of the book each constitute a unit by themselves but are held together by more than a common theme.

In the first place, the entire book is bracketed by the almost identical declarations of meaninglessness in 1:2 and 12:8. Nor is it an accident that the first poem is a prologue serving to introduce the entire volume. The long passage on the "king's" investigation of wisdom and folly (1:12–2:26) is logically first in the series of reflections that follow. This is where the self-presentation of the author and the royal fiction occur, items that are useful only when they are offered at the beginning.

A further indication that the order of the poems is not accidental is the fact that in 3:1–4:16 we encounter seven poems on the idea of time and its manifestations—the ordinary events that human beings experience.

In 5:10–6:9 numerous pronouncements all having to do with the same theme, namely, the worthlessness of riches, have been brought together. The poems of 6:10–8:1 have in common ideas concerning human incompetence and the worthlessness of wisdom. The three passages of 8:10–9:10 concern wisdom and retribution; 9:11–10:11 concerns the worthlessness of wisdom; and 10:12-20 embraces two poems about speech and silence. In his final poem the Preacher exchanges the order "vanity-joy" for the order "joy-vanity" so that the entire book ends where it began—on the dark note of meaninglessness.

From all these givens it is evident that the book has to be called a volume of poetry. The separate poems have not been collected and arranged in random fashion; but neither—as the repetitions and the few independent poems indicate—is there in it an unfolding theme as we would expect in a scientific treatise.

V. THE BACKGROUND OF THE PREACHER'S WISDOM

To understand the full import of the Preacher's wisdom it is necessary for the reader to bear in mind its unique place in the development of the wisdom of Israel. The wisdom of Israel, despite the difference in time, developed through the same phases that Egyptian and Mesopotamian wisdom did. Comparing the development of wisdom in Israel with that in the other two cultures, we discover that it falls exactly into place, like a piece of a jigsaw puzzle.

Egyptian wisdom had a strong religious cast. Creation and life had been ordered by the god Atum. According to the Egyptians, the wise man is he who in his everyday activities seeks to integrate himself harmoniously into this divine order. This is achieved by doing the right thing at the right time. In one Egyptian wisdom passage, for instance, a man is reckoned wise when he has learned "to act in accord with prevailing circumstances." Another passage says, "Food is good in due time; sleep is good when one tires." Right or wrong depends on time and circumstances; by adapting their actions accordingly, people can integrate themselves into life's order.

When these precepts are written down, however, their actual relation to reality is weakened. When the wise man finds himself unable to apply the ancient precepts in accordance with new circumstances, wisdom petrifies into an abstract, rock-hard system. This process is present in the Teaching of Anii, who held up for his son's instruction a system that can be learned but cannot be realized in practice. He expects that his son, "like all animals," will blindly accept and simply obey what he cannot understand. This petrified doctrinal system evokes protest—a crisis arises in wisdom and Anii's son puts his objections into words.

We discover a similar development in Mesopotamia. Here too wisdom teachers were familiar with the idea of a world-and-life order, and for them too that order was a matter of interest to the gods. In the first phase of that development there was the same appreciation for the need to take the right action at the right time, that is, for the connection between wisdom and time with its varying circumstances.

But when scripturally encoded wisdom can no longer be brought into relationship with the realities of situation and time, then a dogmatic system comes into being: reality is compressed into dogma or doctrine. Because this is unsatisfactory, a crisis ensues. We know a number of writings that illustrate this development. Because of their similarity to the Old Testament book of Job (where the issue is the doctrine of retribution) there is mention of "Job literature." The question in this literature is always how to interpret suffering when it comes upon the innocent. The religious order answers that good fortune follows correct behavior and misfortune incorrect behavior. As a solution to the question of retribution, a harsh and petrified code of wisdom proceeds not from a base in reality but from a base in unchanging dogma. If a person suffers, the inference is that this person is a sinner. Even though there is plenty of real-life evidence that there are numerous happy people who have sinned worse than devout people who suffer misfortune, that evidence falls outside the purview of the petrified doctrine, and therefore the doctrine no longer satisfies. The same capitulation of wisdom to the process of petrification is found elsewhere, in a text that declares that the devout sufferer will ultimately be restored. In this way the theory is saved, but there is no recognition of, or solution to, the question how such suffering of an innocent person is even possible in a harmonious world order.

Focusing now on the wisdom of Israel we again run into the three phases—even though there is an enormous time gap between the wisdom literature of the Old Testament and some texts of the surrounding cultures. These three phases are 1) a strong appreciation for the relationship between action and the opportune time for action, 2) a loss of that sense of temporal relevance, so that a dogmatic system originates, and 3) a protest against this petrifaction or fossilization.

Examples of the first phase are plentiful in Proverbs 10–29: a word must be timely (15:23; 25:11); a loud greeting at an inappropriate time becomes a curse (27:14); correct actions are prescribed for specifically described circumstances, for instance, in harvest time (10:5), at the royal court (14:35), in business practice (16:11), or during a meal (23:1-3). By conducting themselves accordingly, people integrate themselves into God's order and can expect harmony in their lives.

But in the following phase there is a process of fossilization in Israel.* Apart from examples in Proverbs, there are the three friends of Job who are exponents of this systematic sort of wisdom. They close their eyes to Job's piety and argue not only that foolish action brings misfortune but that one can

---

*Those who wish to pursue this matter can find material in J. A. Loader, *Polar Structures in the Book of Qohelet* (Hawthorne, N.Y.: De Gruyter, 1979), p. 121.—Trans.

infer from the fact of misfortune that the sufferer has by his actions disturbed the world order. According to their doctrine Job cannot be a truly godly and devout man, even if his godliness is there for all to see. It is against this kind of rigid wisdom that protest arises. The chief spokesmen for the protest movement are Job and the Preacher.

The Preacher agrees with all the "protestants" in the world of ancient Eastern wisdom that fossilization is a real problem for him, and he appreciates the idea of relativity. He differs from them to the extent that the problem is not satisfactorily resolved for him: he never comes to a "happy ending." He goes much further than they in his protests: he labels as meaningless vanity not only the doctrine of retribution but all human efforts at attaining prosperity through wisdom. In all the other examples of protest literature known to us there is relaxation of tension in the end because one or another solution to the crisis is offered. But in Ecclesiastes the tension continues to the end; that is the most important characteristic of the entire book. One element is repeatedly placed in opposition to another, and the frustration resulting from the tension between opposing elements is accentuated. Polarization creates tension, and tension, when continued, means frustration. Examples of this will crop up again and again in the exposition. It is certainly no wonder that the Preacher often states that all things are meaningless.

The development of ancient Eastern wisdom is one aspect of the background needed for an understanding of Ecclesiastes. But more is needed. The religious history of the time must be added to this background in order to help answer the question why the Preacher took this special course.

Since the deportation of Israel in the sixth century B.C., by which the nation was forced into exile, profound changes had occurred in the people's religious outlook. They still worshiped the same God their fathers worshiped, but their God-concept became more impersonal. This was a result of the growing absolute monotheism in this period. In earlier times they took account of only one God; yet they did not think much about the existence of other gods, and so did not deny that existence either. As one can tell from the second part of Isaiah, the situation then changed (Isa. 40:12-26; 41:7, 29; 43:10-12; 44:6-20; 45:5, 21; and other texts). When people acknowledge the existence of only one God, that God no longer needs a proper name to distinguish him from other gods. In the process, a tendency develops to use circumlocutions in place of the proper name Yahweh—a tendency already manifest in Daniel, Job, and certain psalms. In the Greek translation of the Old Testament the proper name for God is rendered by "LORD," and the Jews then began to speak of "Heaven," "the Majesty," and "the Glory." In the course of time these circumlocutions became more and more abstract, for example, "the Presence," "the Name," and "the Word." By this process God seemed increasingly remote. When God becomes very distant, a vacuum is left in the place he used to occupy, creating a situation full of tension. On the one hand faith in God and his exclusive rights is upheld, but on the other there is an emptiness in which God grows distant, impersonal, and inaccessible. This tension can be removed only by filling the emptiness with one thing or another.

The Jews did this by introducing intermediary figures. In the Hellenistic period (the time of Greek influence in the ancient world of the East) there arose a new appreciation for personal religion. To accommodate it intermediaries between man and the superremote God were introduced. It is no wonder, then, that numerous angels and archangels made their appearance. But the tendency to avoid God's proper name led to the personification of the circumlocutions, so that they became semiautonomous entities between God and man. "The Presence" and "the Name" and probably also "the Word," having once referred to God, became semipersonal entities. The same applies to figures like "Wisdom" and "the Spirit." The phenomenon can be clearly observed in religious writings of approximately the same period as Ecclesiastes, for example, the books of Tobit (ca. 200 B.C.), the Ethiopian Enoch and Jesus Sirach (both second century B.C.), and others. This is how Judaism resolved the tension between the growing remoteness of God and the desire to hold on to God.

In this development the book of Ecclesiastes forms a striking exception. To the Preacher, God is the distant and remote One (3:11; 8:17) with whom he cannot even speak (5:2) and whose name he never mentions. God does what he pleases with respect to life and death (3:2-8), happiness (5:19), and misfortune (5:13). God's work is even referred to as the "fate" (2:14) or "destiny" (9:2-3, NIV) that blindly overtakes people without regard to wisdom, folly, or piety. The Preacher is not a Deist who thinks that God has turned his back on the world, but God is to him an inaccessible power. In this respect Ecclesiastes fits the pattern of contemporary literature. But it differs radically from it insofar as the Preacher refuses to fill the vacuum between God and man with all kinds of intermediate persons and concepts. That is why the tension in his mind remains unresolved and why he so persistently declares that all is vanity, meaninglessness, and wind.

The Preacher refuses to resolve the tension because his thinking is basically rooted in two traditions. On the one hand his concern is to make room for human participation in, and profit from, the reality of life and not to strive after the preservation of a variety of systems of wisdom. On the other hand, however, he at the same time withdraws from reality by posing as a dispassionate onlooker and observer outside of reality. Involvement and detachment are polar opposites and hence stand in a relationship of tension to each other. Once we grasp this, it becomes clear why the Preacher offers such vehement criticism of the mainstream wisdom of his day and yet uses and appropriates for himself all the typical forms of expression that characterize that wisdom. Everything in his book is marked by opposites and tensions—from the broad perspectives of the background to the fine subunits of the separate poems.

The whole intent and design can be reproduced as follows:

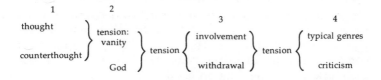

1) The persistent tension in the poems between polar opposites of all kinds leads to 2) the basic theme of vanity, which by itself stands in a relationship of tension to the desire to hold fast to God and also echoes the religious and historical background; 3) this again coincides with the tension deriving from the Preacher's involvement in the wisdom movements of his time; 4) the use of the characteristic genres of that wisdom combined with a critical content in opposition to that wisdom illustrates how polarization suffuses the entire book.

VI. THE SIGNIFICANCE OF THE BOOK AS A WHOLE

Even a cursory reading of the book usually reveals two things. First, the basic mood of the Preacher's thinking is extremely pessimistic—all is vanity. Second, at several places (3:12-13, 22; 8:15; 9:7ff.; 11:7ff.) there appears a call to the enjoyment of life. It is inadequate, however, simply to suppose that the significance of the book lies in the idea that the one should set the limits of the other—in other words, to suppose that the Preacher is concerned to warn both against a black pessimism and against unbridled libertinism, balancing them against each other. For the call to the enjoyment of life always occurs in connection with his conviction of the vanity of things, namely, as the outflow of this conviction. These passages also always refer to the vanity of life and to the fact that since God is the giver of joy he can with equal ease put an end to it. The joy of life is therefore subordinate to the vanity of life, which is riddled with tensions. We will have to acknowledge, then, that there is but one fundamental idea in the book: the declaration of meaninglessness, an idea that is clarified and illustrated from a number of viewpoints. If we were to try to argue this idea out of the picture, we would deprive the book of its basic theological meaning.

For its own time Ecclesiastes had a double significance. The first is the book's total abandonment of the traditional religious concepts of the Jewish people. The total denial of the doctrine of retribution, for instance, is an attack on the very foundations of Judaism. The unvarnished declaration that religious actions, worship, and morality are ultimately irrelevant (9:2-3) is nothing less than a spiritual explosion in the context of the Judaism of the day. The Preacher saw through the weakness of the religion of his contemporaries—its doctrines did not match the reality of life.

The book was also significant because it clearly demonstrated the consequences of the fossilization of wisdom. When wisdom becomes a self-sufficient system, it cannot do justice to the actual problems of life: wisdom's ideas become normative and everything is supposed to accord with a fixed scheme of things, even when reality itself looks very different. Ecclesiastes shows that a reaction to such fossilized wisdom is inevitable and usually ends with an enormous protest. The modern reader is undeniably charmed by the book's penetrating poems and is then confronted with an unavoidable question: Is everything in fact meaningless? When there is an emptiness between God and man, and real alienation has occurred, the answer is yes. The Preacher describes this universal truth and he is right. From the perspective of man everything is in fact meaningless, and man cannot work out his own salvation. Thus the Preacher also indicates how necessary it is that the vacuum be filled if man is to escape the windowless emptiness of his existence. To break through the tension a mediating figure is indispensable. For the Christian this mediator between God and man is the man Jesus Christ.

We can view the Preacher as a painter who offers a realistic portrayal of human life as it looks apart from Christ. The more severe his words, the more terrified the readers are; the more effective his reproduction of life, the more the readers sense their own helplessness. Whether people remain captive to the tensions of meaninglessness or are delivered from them depends on their decision whether or not to accept Christ as the filler of the vacuum. So we can regard the book as a poetic forerunner of the first part of the Heidelberg Catechism—how great our misery is—that cries out, as it were, for a new dispensation: a deliverence from the misery of meaninglessness.

The book is important for the modern reader on still another level. It demonstrates how dangerous such self-sufficient systems are. From this point theology has much to learn. When all the answers can be so easily given, when all is cut-and-dried and people think they have enclosed God within a foolproof system, reaction is inevitable. God and his actions are never the prisoners of fixed patterns, however pious they may be. When theology presents itself to the world with too much self-confidence, and the church has lost the ability to listen to others and just listens to itself, then an unsparing reaction of rejection is bound to come.

The book of Ecclesiastes must, finally, be regarded as one of the most precious possessions of the Christian church. For all those who have been disillusioned by the discovery that the all-embracing systems on which they relied were not in fact reliable, how thrilling and astonishing it is to discover that in Scripture itself a similarly disillusioned and desperate voice may be heard. The numerous people who believe there is a God but do not believe *in* him and the numerous people who are critically opposed to the church and its theology all have a friend in the Preacher of Ecclesiastes, the wise author of a book that is part of the Bible of the church, and therefore they are not totally unchurched.

VII. SUGGESTED LITERATURE

Of the numerous commentaries, monographs, and articles on the book of Ecclesiastes and wisdom literature in general, I have given only a small selection here, with an eye especially to the needs of the general Bible reader.

A. Works on Ecclesiastes

Barton, G. A. *A Critical and Exegetical Commentary on the Book of Ecclesiastes.* The International Critical Commentary. Edinburgh: T. & T. Clark, 1908.

Cochrane, A. Joy to the World: The Message of Ecclesiastes." *The Christian Century* 85 (1968): 27-35.

Eaton, M. *Ecclesiastes: An Introduction and Commentary.* Tyndale Old Testament Commentaries. London/Downers Grove: Inter-Varsity Press, 1983.

Fuerst, W. J. *The Books of Ruth, Esther, Ecclesiastes, The Song of Songs, Lamentations—The Five Scrolls.* The Cambridge Bible Commentary on the New English Bible. Cambridge: Cambridge University Press, 1975.

Ginsberg, H. L. "The Structure and Contents of the Book of Koheleth." In *Wisdom in Israel and in the Ancient Near East.* Ed. M. Noth and D. W. Thomas. Vetus Testamentum 3. Leiden: Brill, 1960.

————. *Studies in Koheleth.* New York: Jewish Theological Seminary of America, 1950.

Gordis, R. *Kohelet—The Man and His World.* 3rd ed. New York: Schocken Books, 1968.

————. *The Wisdom of Ecclesiastes.* New York: Behrman House, 1945.

Hubbard, D. A. *Beyond Futility: Messages of Hope from the Book of Ecclesiastes.* Grand Rapids: Wm. B. Eerdmans Publishing Company, 1976.

Jastrow, J., Jr. *A Gentle Cynic.* Philadelphia: Lippincott, 1919.

Jones, E. *Proverbs and Ecclesiastes.* Torch Bible Commentaries. London: SCM Press, 1961.

Kidner, D. *A Time to Mourn and a Time to Dance.* London/Downers Grove: Inter-Varsity Press, 1976.

Loader, J. A. *Polar Structures in the Book of Qohelet.* Berlin/Hawthorne, N.Y.: De Gruyter, 1979.

Rankin, O. S. and G. G. Atkins. "Ecclesiastes." In *The Interpreter's Bible.* Ed. G. A. Buttrick. New York: Abingdon-Cokesbury, 1956.

Scott, R. B. Y. "Ecclesiastes." *The Anchor Bible.* Vol. 18. Garden City, N.Y.: Doubleday, 1965.

Whitley, C. F. *Koheleth: His Language and Thought*. Berlin/Hawthorne, N.Y.: De Gruyter, 1979.

Williams, J. G. "What Does It Profit a Man? The Wisdom of Koheleth." *Judaism* 20 (1971): 179-93.

B. *Works on Wisdom Literature*

Baumgartner, W. "The Wisdom Literature." In *The Old Testament and Modern Study*. Ed. H. H. Rowley. Oxford: Clarendon Press, 1951.

Blank, S. H. "Wisdom." In *The Interpreter's Dictionary of the Bible*. Ed. G. A. Buttrick. New York: Abingdon Press, 1962.

Crenshaw, J. L. *Old Testament Wisdom: An Introduction*. Atlanta: John Knox Press, 1981.

Irwin, W. A. "The Wisdom Literature." In *The Interpreter's Bible*. Ed. G. A. Buttrick. New York: Abingdon-Cokesbury, 1951.

Murphy, R. E. *Wisdom Literature: Job, Proverbs, Ruth, Canticles, Ecclesiastes, and Esther*. The Forms of the Old Testament Literature. Vol. 13. Grand Rapids: Wm. B. Eerdmans Publishing Company, 1981.

Rad, G. von. *Wisdom in Israel*. Trans. J. D. Martin. Nashville: Abingdon Press, 1972.

Rankin, O. S. *Israel's Wisdom Literature*. 1936. Reprint. New York: Schocken Books, 1969.

Scott, R. B. Y. "The Study of Wisdom Literature." *Interpretation* 24 (1970): 20-45.

————. *The Way of Wisdom in the Old Testament*. New York: The Macmillan Company, 1971.

THE SUPERSCRIPTION 1:1

The superscription, in all probability, is the work of an editor. By this heading he has extended the royal fiction, which really applies only to the long passage 1:12–2:26, to the entire book. Although the expression "son of David" can, in the Hebrew, refer also to "a descendant of David," the intent of the heading is definitely to introduce David's own son, the one whose name is Solomon, as the author of the book. That is entirely in keeping with the tradition as we know it from 1 Kings 3 and 4:29ff. and with the heading of the book of Proverbs. Nor need this understanding of the heading be in conflict with the reference of 1:16 to "all who were over Jerusalem before me," because there had been rulers over Jerusalem other than David—Absalom for a short time and, before David, the Jebusite kings. What is more, such precise details play no role in the type of fiction with which we are concerned here. Concerning the origin of the literary practice of putting wisdom utterances into the mouth of an earlier king, see section II of the Introduction. The influence of this superscription is noteworthy and explains to some extent why for centuries the book was regarded as authoritative and therefore accepted as part of the canon.

THE PROLOGUE 1:2-11

Verses 2 and 3 serve as an introduction to the prologue and simultaneously to the entire book. They announce the basic theme of the volume in such a way that they also lead into the prologue. Verse 2 embraces two exclamations and one assertion. Twice the Preacher cries out, "Vanity of vanities." This is an example of the superlative degree, meaning "total vanity," "complete meaninglessness." By means of the superlative and the device of repetition the Preacher shows that he intends an all-embracing declaration of nullity, and by the assertion "all is vanity" he leaves no doubt whatever that he regards all things as meaningless. Verse 3 then applies this general statement specifically to human actions. It is a rhetorical question; it is not designed to gain information but to posit a thesis. The question, "What does man gain?" therefore means that there is no profit at all in all his labor. It is a statement declaring all human toil "under the sun," that is, in life, to be worthless. His interest is focused on what profits humans in life, and his conclusion is that nothing does. At this point already, then, we are told the final conclusion of the Preacher's reasoning and conviction. The remainder of the prologue will show how he arrived at this pessimistic conclusion, and the rest of the book will illustrate this theme from all angles.

The first thing that gives him cause for pessimism is the transience of man: one generation succeeds another. For one who remembers that it is always the same earth that is the stage for the repeated change from one generation to another, the emphasis on human volatility and transitoriness is heightened. But no one must think that the earth itself is something permanent. There are numerous examples that indicate that the entire creation is subject to the same sort of circular movement and does not produce anything permanent (vv. 5-7).

The sun rises in the morning and sets in the evening, while during the night it has to hasten to its starting point for a new beginning. It does not attain or gain anything by going around and around. It is mere toil, for following its daily journey there is no opportunity for rest to make itself ready for the repeat performance. It is all pauseless, breathless, treadmill-like repetition. The Preacher's pessimistic view of life is so strong it manages to darken even the sun's activity! There is an enormous contrast between this dimming of the most brilliant phenomenon in nature and the picture in Psalms of the sun heroically making its tour of triumph through the heavens (Ps. 19:5-7).

The wind is unable to do better. The northwind blows to the south and then turns around so that the southwind blows to the north. It is as if the wind is ineluctably caught in an endless back-and-forth movement. It moves in a fixed circle— proof that the Preacher fosters an image of the wind very different from that of Jesus (John 3:8): the wind does not blow

20

where it wills but always within fixed channels; you hear its sound and you do know where it comes from and where it is going—from the north to the south and from the south to the north. The wind can never show a profit from its comings and goings; its circular course is senseless.

A third example of meaninglessness in nature is the rivers or streams. The remarkable truth is that although all rivers on earth flow toward the sea, still the sea never gets full. This is a phenomenon about which other people in prescientific antiquity had been astonished. Because they knew nothing of evaporation and condensation, the contemporaries of the Preacher were bound to be impressed by this argument. From our point of view the circular movement of water to the sea and via rain back to the land is meaningful, but to the ancient worldview of the Preacher it is meaningless. For him the idea of repetition lies in that rivers never stop feeding water into the sea; and its meaninglessness lies in that this incessant effort to fill up the sea has absolutely no effect. The effort of the rivers, like that of the sun and the wind, is Sisyphean labor—labor that never accomplishes anything but may not be stopped. And if that is the stage on which the human drama plays, how can we expect man to be able to reverse this senseless sequence.

The second part of the prologue, which focuses on human life, begins at verse 8. The Preacher points out three things that prove that in this domain too there is nothing to be found that is meaningful or permanent.

Wisdom literature's favorite theme, human speech, is the first example. At this point we have to differ from those translations (KJV, RSV, NIV) that speak of all "things" that are wearisome. The Hebrew word at issue sometimes means "things," sometimes "words," but in Ecclesiastes only the latter possibility occurs. Moreover, in the immediate context there is also reference to the ear that hears, implying a specific subject that is under discussion and not a vague concept like "things." All human words are wearisome—just wearisome. There is no possibility of noticing any real change—no distinction between good words and bad words, no difference between the wholesome effect of the first and the bad effect of the latter. It was precisely this distinction that meant so much to wisdom literature in general (cf. Prov. 15:1, 2, 4; and further 15:23; 16:24; 25:11). If the Preacher now sees no benefit in any kind of human speech, that is an indication of his conviction in general and of his opposition to the wisdom of his time. By taking this position he even declares wisdom to be worthless—an opinion we shall encounter frequently in the book. There is not a person in the world who can say anything worthwhile, and the ears are never full of the words they continually have to hear, just as the eyes never get enough of seeing. The reasoning here is the same as that which the Preacher used in his final argument from nature: the rivers have no effect on the sea—why then do they keep flowing? Words have no effect on the hearer—why then do people keep speaking?

The second example of the uselessness of life consists in the repetition of things that happen. There is nothing new in life: that which was before comes back again, and what people used to do, they do again later. Even if people did not realize it and were committed to the opposite view, that is due only to ignorance. For even the things they consider new have existed in earlier times, long before the time of the speaker. For the Preacher this expresses a fundamental conviction on his part to which there is no exception. It is characteristic of him to develop his thinking with absolute consistency and without compromise. For him, therefore, human wisdom and human labor have no meaning: all human effort to create something new is doomed to fail, for what happens in time has been determined before time. This theme recurs through the book. The Preacher would assent to the words of the Dutch poet Willem Bilderdijk, "In the past / Lies the present / In the now what shall become" ("Afscheid," 1810), but with reverse intent. Bilderdijk means that out of past frustration something positive can grow—"(The Trojan fall / built the wall / of robust ancient Rome)"—but the Preacher means that the repetition of the past is the *cause* of present frustration.

Finally, there is a third example: human forgetfulness. This much is clear in any case: among human beings there is no memory of the past. The precise meaning can be construed in one of two ways. The Hebrew words can, on the one hand, be reproduced as follows: "There is no remembrance of men of old, and even those who are yet to come will not be remembered by those who follow" (1:11, NIV). The meaning would then be that man cannot make a name for himself (cf. 7:1) and will be forgotten by later generations. This interpretation would fit perfectly the theme of total meaninglessness, which is the Preacher's central thesis. On the other hand, the two Hebrew words "former" and "later" can also mean "former things" and "later things" instead of former and later men. This would seem to be the better translation, for it would do justice to the connection with the preceding verses: It is no wonder that there are people who still think that there is something new in life (v. 10), because their memory is so short that they do not realize how similar the happenings of all times are. This translation also gives a good sense to the last line of the poem. In distinction from the NIV we do not read here a reference to "those who are yet to come." The sentence structure we find in this verse is like that in 2:16 ("For the wise man, like the fool, will not be long remembered," NIV); so the Preacher says that there is no remembrance of what was or of what is coming—any more than there will be of the very last things. That is a forceful comparison, since the Preacher takes no account of a life hereafter. Theoretically speaking, then, after the very last things have occurred, there will be no one to remember what has happened. History is just not remembered. It is therefore because of the faulty memory of man that he does not see how meaningless life is and that, as the wisdom teachers ever and again try to do, he initiates all sorts of optimistic enterprises that are doomed to fail. Again, the Preacher attacks the foundations of wisdom in general.

These three examples from the realm of nature and the three from the sphere of human life serve the Preacher as support for his assertion that everything is meaningless, and at the same time they constitute his reply to the rhetorical question concerning the profit or gains human beings make in life. The entire picture is without a shred of comfort because there is no purpose in life; no toil produces any results, for man cannot attain anything permanent any more than nature can.

The Preacher has already demonstrated his opposition to current trends in wisdom and also his dissent from a frequently recurring emphasis in the remainder of the Old Testament: a positive appreciation for the divine guidance of history. It is self-evident that such pessimism is unacceptable to those who believe that Christ constitutes the meaning of history and that human labor done in his service is not meaningless. But that very belief implies, as a self-evident corollary, that the Preacher will be on target if we lose sight of Christ.

EXPERIMENTS AND THEIR RESULTS 1:12–2:26

This passage is by far the longest poem in the volume. For that reason alone, but also because "King Solomon" is here presented to the reader, it is understandable that this poem should introduce the collection of reflections between the prologue and the epilogue. The poem can be divided into six parts:

1. After a self-introduction the king tells the story of an experiment he has conducted (1:12-15).
2. The experiment is applied to wisdom (1:16-18).
3. The experiment is applied to folly (2:1-11).
4. The first dimension of the relationship between wisdom and folly: fate (2:12-17).
5. The second dimension of this relationship: the fruits of labor are lost (2:18-23).
6. The effect of God's arbitrary deeds (2:24-26).

1:12-15 THE PROGRAM IS ANNOUNCED

The Preacher starts by announcing that he is "king." So the experiment he has undertaken is a royal experiment. By these means he makes credible the grandly conceived and all-embracing investigation of which the poem tells, for only a king is capable of initiating and carrying out such a costly enterprise. The conclusions to which the Preacher comes must have general validity, so the area to be investigated must be universal, including "all that is done under heaven." So we can see that the royal fiction has a specific literary function; we must therefore accept it as a literary fact and not as a historical reference. The Preacher's work is not only extensive; it is also thorough. It is a matter not only of studying materials over a wide range but also of intensive exploration—and all this "with wisdom." The result is that one can safely conduct one's life by its conclusions.

24

The results of the exploration are already anticipated, however, in the announcement of it. This does not mean that the Preacher has decided before undertaking his study what the outcome would be. But at the very beginning of this report he does announce the conclusion at which he has arrived. The essence of it is that all that is done on earth is an unhappy business with which God burdens men and is therefore meaningless. A more negative judgment of human labor is hardly possible. The conclusion is not only that nothing positive can come from human labor but also that man is inescapably doomed to toil at his senseless and vexing labor because God has laid it on him. This is a clear indication of how the Preacher pictures God: an overwhelming power to which the toil and trouble of life must be attributed. This is also evident from the proverb he cites in support of his argument: "You can't straighten out what is crooked; you can't count things that aren't there" (1:15, TEV).

Things are simply as they are and man cannot do a thing about it. As a rule this fatalism has the effect of shocking the Bible reader, but it is neither possible nor necessary to explain it away. Such ideas are completely understandable at a time when God seems distant to people, and they are wholesome for those who can no longer picture to themselves from what condition they were delivered.

By itself the proverb can also have another meaning. A person experiences certain things in life as self-evident: if something is crooked, it is crooked, and there is nothing one can do about it; and if something is not there, it cannot be noted or counted or recorded. These observations illustrate a valid truth and can be interpreted in a completely positive sense. Here is a student who is eager to make a success of his life; where can he get advice better than that from a teacher who presses his nose into this kind of realism? It is a useful policy for the conduct of one's life to take account of reality. That is how the optimistic teachers of wisdom of that time may have used this proverb. But in the context in which it is used here the proverb is an expression of pessimism; according to it there is no possibility of managing one's life successfully. In other words the Preacher uses a typical form of expression from the wisdom of his day—the proverb—to polemicize against that wisdom.

1:16-18 THE EXPERIMENT APPLIED TO WISDOM

The Preacher now begins the narrative, in the form of an autobiographical discourse, of the judgment of wisdom he has formed in the course of his experiment. He acquired greater and more inclusive wisdom than any of his predecessors in Jerusalem—after all, no one had more wisdom than Solomon. Whatever his findings, they will be very trustworthy. The wisdom and knowledge he gathered up in the course of his observations mean varied and extensive experience and the ability to make decisions. Wisdom here examines itself, then, and comes to a devastating verdict: wisdom and folly are in exactly the same position; both are "a chasing after wind." The experiment with folly does not come until 2:1-11, so there has to be a special reason why madness and folly are mentioned in the report on the experiment with wisdom. That reason has to do with the practice of mainline wisdom literature, which made a ready distinction between wisdom with its good results and foolishness with its bad results. To the teachers of wisdom, no contrast is clearer than that, but the Preacher's point is that ultimately there is no difference between the two. He attacks established wisdom in its very foundations. Mentioning folly at this point serves to bring out the more sharply his negative evaluation of wisdom.

Again the Preacher uses a proverb to underscore his conviction: "The wiser you are, the more worries you have; the more you know, the more it hurts" (1:18, TEV). The combination of wisdom and pain mentioned here is a familiar notion in the wisdom of the schools (e.g., Prov. 13:24; 22:15; and also in Egyptian and Mesopotamian traditions). Gaining wisdom is a painful process and so pain serves a good purpose. However, that is not the sense in which the Preacher uses the proverb. For him the logic of it is precisely the opposite: wisdom increases pain and therefore wisdom serves no good purpose. So it is another instance in which the Preacher enters the fray against the general wisdom teachings of his day.

But if this is what wisdom produces, it makes sense to change the focus of the investigation. For that reason the very opposite of wisdom needs to be considered.

2:1-11 THE EXPERIMENT APPLIED TO FOLLY

Again, the Preacher tells of his test in the form of an autobiographical tale. He has decided on a program of joy and pleasure. We have to be careful at this point not to confuse the meaning of this enjoyment with its meaning elsewhere in the book (3:12-13, 22; 8:15; 9:7-10; 11:7–12:8). Enjoyment here is part of the life-style of the fool (contrasting with the idea that wisdom and pain go hand in hand), but elsewhere in the book it is part of the final conclusion at which the Preacher arrives (one must enjoy oneself to make the best of a hopeless situation). So his concern here is with blind and foolish pleasure and not with his later, well-considered conclusion that sprang from his conviction that everything is worthless. At the very beginning we already heard what his conclusion was: meaningless (v. 1). Laughter is madness and pleasure produces nothing (just as at 1:3, the point is made here at 2:2 by means of a rhetorical question with negative intent).

The details follow. The Preacher enters upon his experiment to the accompaniment of wine and folly. As is frequently the case in the Old Testament, wine is here the symbol of the pleasure of life in general (see Deut. 14:26; Judg. 9:13; Ps. 104:15; Isa. 5:11; and other places). The pronouncement on wine in verse 3 and that on folly are parallel—both occur at the end of succeeding lines of verse. This common feature of Hebrew poetry indicates that there is a close connection between the two parts. By this device pleasure (represented by wine) and folly are equated. The question is, however, whether one who has surrendered himself to drunkenness and folly is able to carry out an experiment. The Preacher is aware of a possible objection to the validity of his conclusions on the grounds that he is incompetent. So between the two pronouncements he inserts a parenthesis: his mind was still guided by wisdom and he was in control of the situation throughout. In other words, he did not surrender his wits to the enjoyments of pleasure and did not become their slave. Just as earlier he used wisdom to examine itself, so he, the wise man, now uses wisdom to examine folly. A similar assurance occurs in verse 9.

In his attempt to establish what is good for man, however, the Preacher embarked on many more projects, for the experiment with folly must be just as thorough as the one applied to wisdom. He paints his life of pleasure in colors that fit a typical king of the ancient East and that, in accordance with the tradition of Solomon's wisdom (1 Kings 3) and the heading of 1:1, reinforce the image of "Solomon the Preacher" (vv. 4-8). His building projects may be compared with the report of Solomon's building activities in 1 Kings 9:10, 15, 17ff. The reference to vineyards, gardens, and parks planted with fruit trees agrees with what we read in 1 Chronicles 27:27-28 concerning the crown possessions of his father David and with the mention of a royal garden in 2 Kings 25:4. Such specially constructed gardens could be watered only with the aid of conduits, to which Nehemiah 3:15-16 refers. The reference to his great herds and flocks again agrees with a similar statement about his father's property (1 Chron. 27:29ff.). Male and female slaves are mentioned in the same breath as herds and flocks because they were simply considered their master's property. Solomon used them for forced labor (1 Kings 9:15-22) and at his court (1 Kings 10:5). His collections of gold and silver were legendary (1 Kings 10:14ff.); indeed Solomon could claim to have gathered together the riches of kings and provinces (1 Kings 10:23-25). Counted among Solomon's personnel were singers, though they served in the temple (2 Chron. 5:13); in a later report, which comes down from the Assyrian king Sennacherib, we read of male and female musicians who were connected with the royal court at Jerusalem. Finally, we learn of the harem, a typical part of every Eastern court in ancient times; with it, too, Solomon gained special renown (1 Kings 11:3). At this juncture we have to differ from the KJV, which skirts around the reference to the women with the vague mention of "the delights of the sons of men" (2:8). The reference is rather to specifically erotic delights, a reference it would have been particularly odd to find lacking in this catalogue of delights. Greater opportunities for the enjoyment of life are hardly conceivable, and the Preacher let himself use them without restriction—preserving his integrity as an experimenter, of course (vv. 9-10).

And when he looks back on all these things, things he has achieved with toil and effort, his judgment is negative (v. 11). Folly in the form of the enjoyment of life is meaningless too. This declaration of futility balances that which was made at the end of the experiment with wisdom (1:17-18). There the Preacher quoted a proverb to indicate, by its ironic effect, the total senselessness of wisdom. Now he uses a three-fold formula to put equal emphasis on the meaninglessness of folly: it was all futile, a pursuit of wind, no use at all.

2:12-17 VIEWING WISDOM AND FOLLY FROM THE PERSPECTIVE OF FATE

The royal researcher now turns his attention simultaneously to wisdom and folly. We encountered this combination already in 1:17, but there its purpose was to polemicize against the wisdom teachers of the time. The purpose here is to examine the relationship between wisdom and folly. Most commentators want to move verse 12b from its present location, but it makes good sense where it is. The Preacher loves to anticipate a topic that will be treated more fully later. In a moment he will show that wisdom and folly are alike when a person dies, and he will give an illustration of how a foolish successor can take over the achievements of his predecessors (vv. 18-23). So here he makes an allusion to those thoughts, but the emphasis lies on the fact that the king's successor, notwithstanding the progression of time, will find himself in the same situation as the king. The exploration of wisdom and folly showed that they shared a common fate. Now the very opposite idea comes tumbling out of the mouth of the same speaker! In verse 13 the Preacher expressly says that wisdom has an advantage over folly, comparable to the advantage that light has over darkness; and in verse 14 we again get to hear a proverb that praises the conventional wisdom of the established teachers: "The wise man has eyes in his head while the fool walks in the darkness" (NIV, cf. Prov. 3:13-14; 13:20).

These images are all congruent: wisdom, light, wise man, eyes in one's head; folly, darkness, fool, walking in darkness. So the wise man surpasses the fool insofar as he can see, while the fool in his blindness goes groping in the dark. But then comes the main point (a visible feature of which is its introduction by an autobiographical notation): the same fate overtakes both, the one who sees as well as the one who does not. And that in turn leads inevitably to the following consequence, namely, that the wise Preacher will incur the same fate as any fool. Therefore, with the aid of his beloved rhetorical technique, he can again call his own wisdom into question. His wisdom was not significant. The value of wisdom is obvious when compared with folly, but its worthlessness is equally obvious when viewed in the light of one's fate. Hence the Preacher has a strong feeling for relativity. His polemic against conventional optimistic wisdom comes through in the theme at which he is working; it comes through also in the manner in which he works at it. When he uses a proverb, as he does here and in 1:15 and 18, that proverb, though it may have its own precise meaning, takes on exactly the opposite meaning when it is incorporated into the critical context of this book. If anywhere in Scripture there is a book that illustrates how dangerous it is to support opinions, arguments, and sermons with a few extracted texts or verses, it is Ecclesiastes.

2:18-23 VIEWING WISDOM AND FOLLY FROM THE PERSPECTIVE OF FRUITLESS LABOR

The subject is still the relationship between wisdom and folly, but now another dimension comes into his field of observation: the aspect of the successor, to which verse 12 has already referred. The Preacher mentions the wealth he has "toiled" for and that he must leave to his successor (v. 18). So the word "toil" refers to the products of his work rather than to the work itself. The knowledge that someone else will enjoy the fruits of his labor makes him loathe the gains he has made. One might think that it is extremely selfish for a man to begrudge his successor the enjoyment of his inheritance, but the issue for the Preacher is that he cannot determine whether his successor will be a wise or a foolish person, not that sooner or later he will have to leave his wealth to another. By toil and wisdom he has made gains, but his successor may well be a fool—and then wisdom has only served the interests of folly. Therefore wisdom is worthless. No wonder despair arises in such a situation; obviously there is no certainty or anchorage in life—almost anything may follow in the wake of wisdom. The official wisdom teachers have taught with conviction that a good result can be credited to wise action and that bad results doubtless issue from foolish action; the book of Proverbs is full of this kind of wisdom. But the Preacher puts an end to all this self-assurance by pointing out that only uncertainty can be counted on.

Verse 21 expands the argument with a variation on the main theme. Not only is the prevailing doctrine made uncertain by the possibility that an inheritance may go to a fool, but it becomes completely unacceptable as a result of the laws of inheritance: a man works hard to achieve something positive with wisdom, knowledge, and competence, but because he cannot live forever there has to come a time when someone else enjoys the gains he has made. It does not even matter whether this successor is wise or foolish; the fact remains that he enjoys something for which he has not worked. And by that token the bottom has been knocked out of the doctrine of retribution with which the prevailing wisdom operates: what sense is there in a system of wisdom that functions on the basis of the misguided principle that wise toil brings with it success and reward? When you take a closer look at the real outcome of each, wisdom and folly are not so far apart from each other. All that wisdom really produces is worry and sleepless nights.

It is clear from the experiments of the Preacher, and from his subsequent reasoning, that a penetrating eye and a keen intellect set him apart. He is not content with superficialities and easy answers; he goes to the bottom of an issue. This acuteness of mind is also visible in the techniques he uses to construct his poems. Apart from the proverbs with their double meanings, of which we have now run into several, his love of symmetry provides additional and significant proof of literary skill. The declaration of futility that marks the book is used with regularity in this part of the poem: first after four lines of verse (v. 19), then after three (v. 21), and then after two (v. 23).

2:24-26 THE EFFECT OF GOD'S ARBITRARY DEEDS

The final part of the poem begins with a statement that strikes some commentators as so strange that they want to change the Hebrew text. For the Preacher says in so many words that it is *not good for a man* to eat and to drink and to afford himself enjoyment for all his toil.* Because in another place

---

*The author's translation of 2:24 begins, "It is not good that man should eat and drink and give himself to enjoyment in his toil" (cf. RSV, NIV, etc.).—Trans.

he says practically the opposite (cf. 3:12, 22), the commentators think something has to be inserted at the beginning to bring the meaning of the sentence into line with later pronouncements. But there is not a single reason for this. The point here is not that the Preacher's pessimism brings him to a conclusion that makes pleasure the most desirable option; the point is to illustrate the incalculability of God's interventions in human life. This becomes plain when we look at the matter in retrospect.

Verse 26 links wisdom with enjoyment: God gives them to whomever he wants. On someone who displeases him he lays the task to amass wealth for another—which, in the light of verses 18-23, may be the fate of the wise man as well. So a person may receive from God either joy or frustration. God is bound to no rule, and wisdom has nothing to do with whether a person is fortunate or unfortunate. It all depends on God's unpredictable and totally arbitrary pleasure. In view of the uncertainty that this fact produces, it is no wonder that the declaration of futility recurs here. This also explains the meaning of the rhetorical question in verse 25. No one can eat apart from God and no one can think apart from God. He is the apportioner both of "eating" (the idea of enjoyment) and of "thinking" (the idea of wisdom). Therefore it is not good that people should eat and drink and enjoy themselves as a matter of course, for if these things come from God, then they are subject to his unpredictable wishes that can change at any moment. In light of what follows, verse 24 refers expressly to the kind of thoughtless enjoyment that takes no account of the unreliability of fate. Just as God can give or take away the pleasure of eating and drinking, he can give or take away wisdom. For that reason not only the results of wisdom are uncertain, but even the possession of wisdom lies outside the control of man.

Summary

The extensive experiments of the Preacher produced negative results: both wisdom and folly are worthless. But when the two are compared, the Preacher finds that wisdom has a degree of priority. But in relation to everything that can happen in human life wisdom proves to be no better than folly. The foundational thoughts therefore operate with a pattern of polar opposites.

Thought:	Generally accepted wisdom
Counterthought:	Folly
Tension:	*Relative* priority of wisdom

And

Thought:	Generally accepted wisdom
Counterthought:	Life's happenstances
Tension:	Worthlessness of wisdom

When Christians are told that wisdom is worthless, they can accept this notion only in a certain sense. They know that human wisdom cannot deliver them from the disturbances, pain, and anguish of life. Insight into what is crooked or untenable no more brings about its removal than a human being can call into being things that do not exist. At this point lies the wholesome element of the Preacher's cultural pessimism—he frightens the overconfident. For the modern-day believer it is not overly hard to accept the Preacher's judgment concerning folly as described in this poem. It is relatively easy to read the depiction of life's pleasure as a condemnation of libertinism. But then we shall have to be honest enough to acknowledge that the relative preference of wisdom over folly, and hence of responsible human conduct, means something different for us than for the Preacher. For him the relative preference of wisdom over folly is provisional, and the ultimate worthlessness of it definite. But when God himself has overcome this absolute human impotence in every area of life, then wise (i.e., responsible) action is again meaningful. In this new sense, which according to the Christian faith has been given to life by Christ, the pessimism of the Preacher is turned upside down. Thus his real value appears: he has portrayed life without Christ.

THE GRIP OF TIME 3:1-9

This passage is one of the most ingenious parts of the Old Testament. Its beauty lies in the absolute symmetry of the entire poem and the precise balance of every pronouncement. This precision is not hard to understand—the Preacher can say grand things simply.

The first and last verses are obviously not cast in the same mold that the rest of the poem is. In verses 2-8 every line has two pronouncements concerning "a time for *x* and a time for *y*." Verse 1, which is more general in content, therefore has to be the heading that gives a summary of the theme of the passage. Verse 9 has a totally different form and has to be the conclusion in which the Preacher, in his own characteristic way, uses a question to posit a thesis. So our attention is directed especially toward the fourteen parallel lines in between.

Each of the Bible verses consists of two poetic verses or lines. Each of these lines consists of two halves, the one half stating the opposite of the other (e.g., planting versus uprooting, killing versus healing), and the two lines that occur together in one Bible verse run parallel to each other. Each statement concerns a "favorable" or an "unfavorable" matter. Now the Preacher so arranges the favorable and the unfavorable pronouncements that they continually relate to each other in an X-pattern (chiasmus). The lines of verse 2 begin, for example, with two favorable pronouncements ("to be born" and "to plant") and end with two unfavorable ones ("to die" and "to pluck up"). But in verse 3 the order is reversed: two unfavorable matters ("to kill" and "to break down") are followed each time by a favorable one ("to heal" and "to build up"). The poem continues and we get the following pattern (F: Favorable, U: Unfavorable):

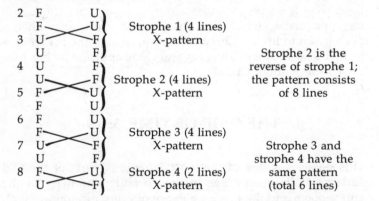

This elaborate pattern makes the poem resemble a modern sonnet. The sonnet also consists of fourteen lines, of which the first eight (octave) comprise two quatrains (strophes of four lines each), and the last six, a quatrain and a couplet (strophe of two lines). It pays to note the precise attention to detail that marks the work of the Preacher, for that shows the penetration of his thought. This passage recounts 28 phenomena, which could be a dull list; this is prevented by the interesting way in which they are arranged. The meticulous attention to the X-pattern, however, has still another function: it emphasizes that things are put in positions of tension with each other.

This poem is one of the very few parts of the book of Ecclesiastes that are generally known. But very often it is misunderstood, too. As a rule, the error arises from mistaking these pronouncements for prescriptions. That the Preacher does not *prescribe* but only *describes* is readily apparent when we look at some of those pronouncements. How could he possibly command a woman to give birth to a child at a given time? Or say that, from a moral point of view, the time has come to die? What sense does it make to tell ordinary people to see to it that war will break out? Thus we see that the Preacher is not saying what people ought to do; he is simply describing the situations they end up in. The entire poem, from verse 1 to verse 9, can be understood on this assumption.

The heading, both in form and content, is most appropriate. Here, too, the X-pattern surfaces (all, time; time, all); the Preacher says there is a time for everything. This cannot mean that there is a correct time to do everything, so the only alternative is that the word *time* has to mean something else. The word can in fact mean "occasion"; then the point at issue is not time as such but the content that fills time. For everything under heaven (everything that happens) there is then a specific occasion. When the occasion arrives, the event that fits it occurs. That is a deterministic view according to which fate has fixed all things in advance and there is nothing anyone can do about it. In harmony with this view is the regular repetition of the word *time* that occurs 28 more times; it sounds like a clock that, inexorably and independent of the wishes of people, keeps ticking and striking. Whatever happens happens, and there is nothing you can do about it.

The Preacher starts his list with those events within which human life is enclosed—birth and death. At a predetermined moment life begins; and when a man's time has come, death takes over. A person has no more choice at death than he or she had at the time of birth. This idea is further qualified by the parallel line in verse 2. The actions of planting and uprooting refer to agriculture. Planting parallels life beginning; uprooting parallels life ending.

Similarly, there is a time at which people kill each other and another time at which they do the precise opposite and devote themselves to healing the sick. Since the Preacher is not saying what people ought to do, we need not worry our heads over the question whether verse 3a concerns murder or "lawful" manslaughter, say in wartime or as part of a judicial procedure. The text does not concern itself with it. Again, a parallel follows in verse 3b. There comes a time in which people tear down and a time in which they build. This may refer to the demolition of houses and their construction; it may also be figurative. In the Old Testament the words for tearing down and building up are often used with reference to the destruction and building up of a human life (see Job 16:14; Gen. 16:2). In that case the first line in verse 3 is expanded by the second.

In verse 4 we have a clear example of how the pronouncements of the first line are made more intense by the second. Sometimes there is occasion for people to weep, and sometimes there is occasion for people to laugh. Weeping represents sorrow, and laughter represents joy; but sometimes sorrow becomes intense and joy exuberant. At the time of a death there is occasion for people to mourn and wail; when other circumstances come their way, people are so happy that they not only laugh but even dance for joy (cf. Ps. 114:4, 6 where the same verb occurs).

What is meant by casting stones and gathering stones (v. 5)? People have thought the reference was to pebbles used by merchants for adding up accounts, stones used in slings, the accumulation or removal of stones on fields, and even to certain funeral practices. But there is another interpretation that does justice to the entire context in which the statement occurs. There is an age-old Jewish interpretation of the book that correctly reports that "casting away stones" refers to sexual intercourse. Gathering stones then means that a man abstains from intercourse with a woman. In each instance the imagery is clear [cf. "the time for making love and the time for not making love," TEV]. Corresponding to this meaning is the mention in the next line of the embrace, which is used as a toned down expression for the same thing (which in fact was the case in the ancient East). So the parallelism between the two lines of a verse, a parallelism maintained throughout the poem, is kept. It would have been odd if it had not been. But the casting away of stones has to have a favorable meaning, unless the finely spun net of the poem was ignored, which would be equally strange. And in fact it was true that abstinence from sexual intercourse took place in times of mourning, hence in unfavorable circumstances (cf. 2 Sam. 12:24 and 1 Chron. 7:21-23). So the opposite situation was a favorable time in which normal relations could again take place. This explanation also fits well after verse 4, where the reference is to the time of mourning and its opposite.

In verse 6 the positive pronouncements again come first and the negative second, as was the case in the first strophe. As in all the other lines, the opposites are mutually exclusive: seeking is the opposite of giving up, and keeping is the opposite of throwing away. The words of the second pair again imply an intensification of the first: "keeping" as compared with "seeking," "throwing away" as compared with "giving up."

At first glance the two lines of verse 7 seem unconnected, but in reality they also parallel each other. The beginning words of each line relate to mourning practices. When in the time of the Old Testament people mourned the death of a loved one, they tore their clothing (cf. Gen. 37:29; 2 Sam. 1:11) and kept silent (cf. Lev. 10:1-3; 2 Kings 2:3, 5; Job 2:13). When the period of mourning was over, clothes could be mended, and the ordinary conversations of the day could continue. So the unfavorable occasions are contrasted with favorable ones. People act in conformity with these occasions but cannot do anything about the caprice with which they come.

In conclusion there is the couplet of verse 8. Here love and peace are placed in a cross pattern, as are hate and war. And again we observe the parallel. The concurrence of these words indicates that the love intended here is nonerotic and general. The other member of the pair, peace, means not only the absence of war but also perfect harmony. On the other hand, war is an intense form of hatred.

This, then, is what human life looks like. On one side is the pole of life and well-being (F) and on the other the pole of death and loss (U). Just as the poem continually moves like a shuttle from one extreme to the other, so the contrasting occasions of life simply befall the people who are subject to them. The Preacher does not advise the reader how people can leap, as it were, from one favorable occasion to the other. And so he ends with the question to which he expects a negative answer: the worker does not profit from all his labor because favorable or unfavorable occasions come over him as a result of fate, quite regardless of his wisdom. By making this point the Preacher again attacks the very core of the prevailing wisdom. The aim of wisdom teachers throughout their working lives was to exclude the negative poles, as it were, by teaching their disciples to make smart choices. But according to the Preacher this attempt to control life was hopeless.

Summary

Thought: Life, well-being
Counterthought: Death, loss
Tension: Abandoning defenseless humanity to the happenstances of life

In this regard we can again be in agreement with the Preacher. No matter how advanced the development of human capacities, science, and technology may be, man cannot guarantee his own happiness. But there is also something very unsatisfactory about the poem. There is a restlessness like that of a weaver's shuttle in it, a persistent uncertainty in the back-and-forth movement of its ideas. It is a restless and unfathomable sea in which the human lifeboat tosses about. Rest is possible only at anchor—and that is what the gospel of Christ offers.

From this perspective the negative experiences of life gain another dimension. According to the Preacher the arbitrariness of God is responsible for the disasters and troubles of human life. But if God is love he does not cause times of hatred, suffering, and war. True, he permits them—we do not know why, any more than Job did—but he is not their cause or author. He is a mighty fortress and refuge especially for the people who threaten to go under in the tensions of life.

THE FUTILITY OF THOUGHT 3:10-15

By means of the formula of observation "I have seen," the author begins a new poem, but there is a connection with the preceding passage. The inscrutable succession of vital occasions, of which we heard in verses 1-9, is here charged to God's account. From this we can tell that the poems in the book have not been strung haphazardly together but have been arranged meaningfully.

The structure of this poem is also noteworthy. The centerpiece concerning the value of the joy of life (vv. 12-13) is enclosed by two sections dealing with the inscrutability of God's work (vv. 10-11 and 14-15). A similar concentric structure occurs in 10:2-7. The Preacher begins with the formula of observation so characteristic of him, telling us what he has seen in life (cf. 1:14; 2:13; 3:16-22; 4:1, 4, 15; etc.). He says he has seen the toil with which human beings torment themselves. But he adds a further pronouncement that though not part of his observation flows from it by way of conclusion: man's toiling is a burden God has laid on him. In this way the torments and troubles man incurs in his labor are charged to God. If it is God who has laid them on man, the suffering inherent in work cannot be escaped. In Ecclesiastes there is no sign of a positive appreciation for work as a way of exercising dominion over the world (cf. Gen. 1:28); nor is there to be found in it a deliberate interpretation of toil as God's punishment upon sin (cf. Gen. 3:17-19).

Although God is responsible for the burdens man carries, there is nevertheless something very fascinating in human life. God is the creator of all things and so he has to be the author of the remarkable succession of things described in the previous section. Therefore the Preacher remarks that God has made everything beautiful "in its season." He does not say it is "good," as Genesis 1:13 does, but "beautiful," admirable. That everything is predetermined shows there is a cause behind it. In everything that happens there is some kind of order that fascinates us. And fascinating it is, for God forces man to occupy himself with the temporal world order by putting it in his heart. In the thought world of the Old Testament the heart was considered the organ of reflection, not of emotion as with us. If then God has set the temporal world order in

39

the human center of reflection, that means he forces man to occupy himself, in his mind, with the unceasing succession of the fixed dispensations of fate that come upon him. But there is a problem: of all the things God does, man understands absolutely nothing. From beginning to end there is not a single aspect human beings can comprehend. So to the Preacher the whole situation is absurd. Man cannot escape the torment of his fate, for God has made it a part of his nature to think about it; yet he gains nothing from all his reflections because God's work remains his own mystery.

In the centerpiece (vv. 12-13) the Preacher draws a perfectly intelligible conclusion from his convictions. He has come to see that in such circumstances there is only one possible life-style: making the best of the prevailing circumstances. Joys and pleasures at least soften the hard edges of the burdens and pains of a meaningless life. But even this tiny ray of light is subject to dark uncertainty. For, says the Preacher, all eating and drinking, all the ordinary enjoyments of life, are gifts from God. By this statement he reminds the reader that God can take them away at any moment.

Some interpreters believe that this pronouncement of verse 13 is so contrary to the Preacher's general pessimism, and especially to the fatalistic picture he presents in the immediate context of God's government of human life, that we have to regard it as a later interpolation by someone else who wanted to soften these hard words. But that is not at all necessary. For if it is God who determines the events of life he can let a time of laughter follow a time of weeping, and at any moment he can turn a time of joy into a time of mourning. So the reference to the unpredictable God is quite in keeping with the context. Further, it is characteristic of the Preacher to refer to the joy of life in a context of uncertainty and pessimism. Rather than a softening of the language the reference to God as the apportioner and dispenser of life is a warning. What all this comes down to is that man had better enjoy himself as long as he can—before the opportunity passes—but must never lose himself in pleasure. So his view of pleasure is anything but shallow; quite the contrary, it is well thought through and therefore demands of his readers deep reflection and seriousness.

The last two verses again tie in with the first two. This structure fits the contents: joy in life, according to the Preacher, can only be a sort of intermezzo in a meaningless life. In keeping with this view the verses that concern joy are set parenthetically between other verses that underscore the meaninglessness of life. It is very different with God who is the apportioner of everyone's lot in life. His actions endure and humans cannot change them in any way whatever. The determinism of the Preacher could not be put into words more clearly than that. No matter what a man tries to do he cannot add a favorable event to God's determinations of life or subtract an unfavorable one. God's dispensations are such that human beings stand in awe of him. This fear of God is not a form of piety; it is terror and a shrinking from him. No other possibility exists in the face of a power that man cannot affect and does not understand. The idea of the circular course of things, familiar to us from the prologue, comes back in the last verse of the poem. God controls life by recycling everything that was before. By this thought the Preacher underscores the unalterable and hopeless abandonment of man to whatever happens.

Summary

Thought:	The incomprehensible, fixed temporal order (life)
Counterthought:	The obligation and pressure to think about it (toil)
Tension:	All human labor is meaningless
Conclusion:	Enjoy life whenever possible

When the Preacher pictures human thought and human labor as absurd, that view stands over against the conclusion he draws from it: be joyful. At first glance it may seem those two thoughts hold each other in balance, as though the futility theme and the joy theme temper one another. But things are not that simple here. The enjoyment to which the Preacher looks forward is the *result* of his conviction that everything is meaningless through and through; it is the consequence of despair that underscores the frustration that lies at its heart.

The Preacher's conclusion of joy is strongly reminiscent of Paul's words when he writes to the Corinthians: "If the dead are not raised, 'Let us eat and drink, for tomorrow we die' " (1 Cor. 15:32). There is a big difference, however: Paul makes the eat-and-drink exhortation dependent on a condition that, in his mind, is not fulfilled whereas for the Preacher it is certain that no other conclusion can be drawn from life's pain. If there is no prospect beyond the grave, then all that remains for man is to enjoy himself as long as he can. The Preacher's conception of history is that of an impenetrable circle of events. Man is underway without direction or goal; he has no destination. Consequently the Preacher has no future expectations. In that respect Paul could assent to the Preacher's conclusion, for without the future of Christ no other posture is in fact conceivable. On the other hand Paul also declares that in his time the conception of the Preacher is no longer tenable because the occasion for it has disappeared in the time between the ministries of the two preachers. When the resurrection of Christ broke through the endless circular movement of history, a direction and a destination was set for human life. Labor then becomes meaningful because in the new circumstances it becomes *service*. The Preacher is valuable because, in his own negative way, he testifies to these things. He was not so mistaken in his judgment, nor did he turn the truth upside down in everything! On the contrary, his reproduction of reality is a reliable sketch of what life is really like apart from Christ.

INJUSTICE INSTEAD OF JUSTICE 3:16-22

This poem, like 3:10-15, has an interesting structure. The first three lines (v. 16) spell out the problem; next come three more lines (v. 17) that appear to solve the problem; and finally the problem is taken up again and expanded (vv. 18-21). The conclusion to enjoy oneself follows, as in the previous poem.

The Preacher starts with an observation he has made in life ("under the sun"). It concerns the area of jurisprudence where the right is subverted: where justice ought to triumph, injustice is found. To the Preacher that is a serious matter, as is evident from his repetition of the statement in almost identical words. It is an immoral state of affairs, one that was earlier encountered in the national household by the prophets of Israel, who forcefully opposed the immorality in the name of God (e.g., Isa. 1:16-17; Jer. 22:3; Amos 3:10; Mic. 2:1; etc.). But what is the reaction of the Preacher?

He says that God will bring to judgment both the person who is right and the one who is wrong in his legal actions. It would seem that at least in this case the Preacher takes a positive position. Does this not mean that the corrupt legal practices of men will be corrected by the judgment of God? If that were the case, the Preacher would have done what the great critical prophets did; furthermore, he would have expressed his agreement with the fundamental doctrine of wisdom literature in general, namely, that "chickens will come home to roost." Indeed, by itself the Preacher's pronouncement about judgment can have that meaning and can appear to affirm wisdom literature. For that reason some interpreters regard it as a later insertion by an editor who attempted to give the words of the Preacher a more orthodox coloring (the same reasoning that is applied to propose editorial changes in 2:25 and 3:13). But again, it is a sample of the fine sensitivity of the Preacher and not of the obtuseness of a later editor. The case is that in the specific context of the poem the words cannot have the meaning they have by themselves.

Verse 17 proceeds to explain why a judgment will befall both the righteous and the unrighteous: there is a time for every activity—for the injustice now practiced and for the judgment of God. But the verses immediately following concern the fate of death, which strikes equally the most diverse of living creatures. So the judgment of God over the two parties at law can refer only to death, which comes over both without discrimination. Moreover, God's judgment does in fact come over both; there is not a single indication in the text that the judgment of one would be favorable and that the judgment of the other would be unfavorable. And that is how injustice in the world is "solved": all die the same death and are placed on the same level by death so that right or wrong simply play no role for the parties who have died. Some comfort! What an utterly unsatisfactory situation if the oppressed person hears only that he too, like the oppressor, will die! When the Preacher stands eye to eye with the same corrupt conditions the prophets raged against, he registers no protest whatever against the oppressors. He simply describes how hopeless life is. The only protest he registers is directed against the general wisdom of the day and the doctrine of retribution at its heart. The Preacher takes it over and smashes it to smithereens by putting it into the context of his own thoughts.

But this is still not the whole story. The irony of retribution by death is heightened even more. The Preacher makes plain the purpose of this judgment: God wants to "sift" men (v. 18)—is that not what happens in a judicial process? A distinction is made between good and evil, right and wrong, innocent and guilty—at least that is what the wisdom teachers think (cf. Prov. 10:7). But the Preacher says that by doing this God only demonstrates that in essence people are animals. Just as animals are not rewarded for practicing justice nor punished for practicing injustice, so people must not expect that God will reward the "righteous" or punish the "wicked." The result of the sifting process, then, is not only that people are of equal worth among themselves but also that people are of no higher worth than animals. By taking this position the Preacher has knocked the foundation out from under the Jewish religion. If no distinction can be made between the righteous and the wicked, then it makes no sense to keep the law, and with that the whole religion collapses.

If in principle there is no distinction between man and animal, then one may expect that there will be no difference in their final fate either. Verses 19-21 are devoted to the accentuation of this idea. Man and animals have the same breath and the same life principle, so man dies just like the animal—with regard to their eternal destiny there is no difference between the two. By drawing that conclusion the Preacher has also lopped the future off the Jewish religion. It is no wonder that some in certain Jewish circles attempted to get out from under the offense of these words. They have said that this pronouncement comes not from the Preacher "Solomon" but from a fool. But, as throughout the book, we cannot now explain away the difficulties the Preacher presents to us. Mercilessly he continues the argument: the destination of all living things is the same. This is an obvious reference to death, for in a parallel statement there is an allusion to the Paradise story:

Ecclesiastes 3:20	*Genesis 3:19*
"all come from dust, and to dust all return"	"for dust you are and to dust you will return"
(NIV).	(NIV).

Not only in the choice of words but in the thesis itself the Preacher here borrows from the first book of Moses. In the Paradise story man is referred to in the same way animals are: both are living beings and both were made from the dust of the earth (Gen. 2:7, 19). Further, God himself says that man returns to the earth at death simply because he was originally taken from the ground (Gen. 3:19). If then man and animal share the same origin there is no reason why they should be different in death. If that were not the case, one would in fact expect that animals would meet with a better fate than people, for only people are expressly condemned to return to the dust. This alternative is even worse than the conviction the Preacher holds. So there is no escape for his opponents, who adhere to a traditional viewpoint. Is there anyone who wants to oppose this reasoning perhaps? Then he had better be prepared to take up the fight against the first book of holy Scripture as well, for that, as the Preacher subtly and characteristically hints, is his basis. Thus he takes away from the more traditional view of his contemporaries every basis for appeal.

A final emphasis follows when the Preacher asks his favorite rhetorical question to counter traditional understanding: "Who knows whether the spirit of man goes upward and the spirit of the animal downward?" The assumed answer is that no one can be sure. The ancient Hebrew view of the underworld was that man has to lead a ghostlike existence in the realm of the dead. But in a later age the idea of heaven as the dwelling place for the righteous broke through in Israel, too. It is against this notion that the Preacher now takes up arms. There is, according to him, no evidence that people will meet a higher destination after death than the animals do.

While the belief in the vanity of life led him to the conclusion that people should enjoy themselves as best they may, the idea that there is nothing to look forward to on the other side of the grave gives even more impetus to that conclusion. Consequently he calls on his readers to make use of every occasion for joy as long as it is there (v. 22). The word *portion* (KJV) suggests that someone is the apportioner, and as we saw in the previous poem that is the inexplicable God. The Preacher asks: Who knows what awaits us after death? No one, naturally. Then make the best of what lies within your field of experience. This idea is not unique; everywhere in the ancient world we encounter examples of the cry, "Let us eat and drink and be merry, for tomorrow we shall be dead."

This entire train of thought proceeded from the Preacher's observation that there is injustice in life. Injustice takes place even where justice is expected. When these two poles stand as opposites there is only one "solution"—death. Human beings then end up no better than animals, and if we human beings and animals are equal in death, is that not a bitter way of saying that oppressors and the oppressed are also equal?

Summary

Thought:	Justice
Counterthought:	Injustice
Tension:	Death without an afterlife as "comfort"
Conclusion:	Enjoy yourself whenever possible

This thought frightens not only the traditional listeners from the days of the Preacher; it causes us to shrink from it as well. Is there then no meaning inherent in the ideal of justice? Is man of so little importance that oppression does not matter? One's view of justice depends on one's view of man. Justice plays no role in deciding which sheep are led to the slaughterhouse and which are taken into green pastures. And if in essence man is no more than an animal, justice plays no role in his life either. This shakes the foundations of the self-aware modern man who so readily overestimates his own worth and possibilities.

But for all the appreciation with which we regard this provocative material, we cannot be satisfied with this one-sided negative view of human worth. Are there no other values in the opening chapters of holy Scripture than those to which the Preacher refers? Is man not also the imagebearer of God, and is it not his task to rule over the animals (Gen. 1:26)? Has God not made man "almost divine" (Ps. 8:5)? Although on the one hand man is puny and small, on the other he is still of great value.

For that reason Christ became man: man is so precious to God that he sent his Son to overcome a futureless death. The Preacher's argument no longer holds. We now view man's insignificance from another perspective—it no longer leads him to give up all hope; rather it confers the insight that God cares about the insignificant. For that reason one can no longer remain unmoved at the sight of injustice in the world. If God cares about the insignificant, we too will have to take their cause to heart.

The things we observed about the theme of joy at the conclusion of the previous poem apply no less here, especially because the idea of death and destiny is so prominent. If Christ rose from the dead, man's joy takes on a different color. Instead of rejoicing merely to escape life, it now becomes possible to enjoy life itself because there is a meaningful destination at the end of it.

OPPRESSION AND THE OPPRESSED 4:1-3

This short poem consists of two distinct parts. The three lines of verse 1 distill what the Preacher has observed in life, and the remaining three lines contain the conclusion to which he has come on that basis. The theme is closely related to that of the previous poem; here too, the concern is with justice and death. It is no accident, therefore, that the two poems stand back to back.

In the first half the Preacher says he has seen *all* the oppression that is taking place in life. This is a sign that he is not giving a literal account of what has really happened, for there is no way he could have observed every act of injustice in the world. Yet he wants to claim that he has covered all instances so that his view about oppression may apply to all cases without exception. On one side there are always the oppressed who weep, and on the other, the oppressors. But there is no one to comfort those who weep. The Hebrew text shows that power proceeds from the oppressors, hence that they use their power against the oppressed. The Preacher's point, then, is not just that there are powerful persons in the world but that power corrupts. The repetition of "and there was no one to comfort them" shows how utterly hopeless the lot of the oppressed is. There is in these words something sadly sonorous as if the author's sympathy is on the side of the oppressed. We cannot say more—there is obviously no protest against oppression, only a sketch of social reality.

On this basis the Preacher draws his conclusion (vv. 2-3):

if this is what life is like, death has the advantage. So he praises the advantage the dead have over the living. Yet that is surely no comfort since the Preacher has no expectation of an afterlife. So we have here another instance of irony, as in the preceding poem—the hardness of life is met with comforting words that provide no comfort. It is often pointed out that similar thoughts are expressed in Jeremiah and Job (Job 3; Jer. 20:14-18), but in those passages there is an important difference. Job and Jeremiah speak from the impulses of deep emotion; their acts of cursing the gift of life are explosions of bitterness felt in deep anguish. The Preacher, however, is speaking calmly and after deep thought; for him the issue is a general principle. Death is no escape to a better world; that is evident from the last verse. Those who have never been born are better off than both the living and the dead. Nonexistence is by far the most preferred state; someone who has never existed has never suffered the evil that takes place either. Such a statement must have sounded very strange to the ears of a true Israelite, because in Israel the birth of children was always a joyous event and a great blessing. When the Preacher praises death as being better than life he is not contradicting what he says in 9:4 (cf. 3:2), for in the latter instance his intention is ironic. No one could put the futility of life and the dead-end despair of man in words more bitter than these.

The theme of social justice occurs not only in the great prophets but throughout the Old Testament. Wisdom literature is no exception to this rule, and in Proverbs we find remarkable concern over the lot of the poor in society (e.g., Prov. 14:31; 17:5; 19:17; 21:13; 22:22-23). Though the Preacher may have some feeling for such people, he does not move a muscle to change their lot. He just stands by, watching. By this posture of the bystander he demonstrates that he differs not only from the great prophets who lived centuries before but also from the teachers of wisdom. In the process the subject of social justice becomes for him just another opportunity to illustrate the emptiness of life and at the same time yet another opportunity to attack the general wisdom of his day.

Summary

Thought:	Sufferers
Counterthought:	Oppressors
Tension:	Helplessness (an empty life)

The Preacher's powerful thoughts, like a strong sea current, tug us into his world. Reading them, one experiences something of how a drowning person, without ground beneath his or her feet, must feel: completely subject to the pull of death, a death that offers no solution to our difficulties. But in this manner the Preacher confronts us with the question whether the world still looks to us as he presents it. The answer is no. A Savior has appeared to bring us back to solid ground. If Christ had not come, the conclusion of verses 2 and 3 would have been correct. To put it in the slightly different words of Paul, had Christ not overcome death we would be "of all men most to be pitied" (1 Cor. 15:19). But if this then is true, we cannot remain inactive spectators of a life devoid of comfort. If one's destination changes from being devoid of comfort to being rich in comfort, the journey toward it changes from being devoid of meaning to being full of meaning. So all those whose tears God will wipe away in the coming time (Rev. 7:17) now have the task of wiping away the tears of the oppressed. They are now responsible for comforting those who have no one else to comfort them.

THE WORTHLESSNESS OF LABOR (1) 4:4-6

The poems of verses 4-6 and 7-12 both concern the subject of labor, but the perspective is not the same. In the first instance human labor is viewed from the perspective of envy; in the second, from the perspective of solitariness.

As he loves to do, the Preacher reports that he has made an observation. Again it is an all-embracing observation that, as we saw in the preceding poem, must not be taken literally. He cannot possibly have seen *all* toilsome labor or *all* skillful enterprise in the world, but he can maintain the fundamental conviction that all human labor suffers from the same fault. That, in fact, is what he says in verse 4. He makes his judgment without any qualifying words to soften it: all labor, and all competence or skill demonstrated in connection with it, is worthless and devoid of meaning. This does not mean that the Preacher is advising his followers to stop working and to go on a permanent strike as a protest against life (cf. 9:10), but it does mean that according to him there is no real value in working.

We can tell that this is what he means from the proverb that follows (v. 5), one that could equally well have been a part of the wisdom of the book of Proverbs. In that tradition a contrast is often made between laziness and diligence, the one getting criticism and the other praise (e.g., Prov. 10:4; 12:24; 18:9; 19:15; 20:13). On this view slothfulness is a form of folly that results in poverty. But now it is the Preacher who says it. Compare the statements of Proverbs 6:10-11 and 24:33-34 with the poem before us:

Ecclesiastes 4:5	*Proverbs 24:33b-34a*
"The fool folds his hands and ruins himself" (NIV).	". . . a little folding of the hands to rest, and poverty will come upon you like a robber."

The folding of the hands is a sign of laziness; the result is a loss of income, so that the fool ruins himself ("to eat one's own flesh" [RSV] is a Hebrew expression that means that the flesh of the sluggard wastes away because of his laziness or that for lack of food he eats his own flesh; cf. Ps. 27:2). A moment ago the Preacher denied that labor was valuable, and now he shows the opposite attitude by criticizing laziness. In this instance also many commentators have considered the verse irreconcilable with the general tenor of the book and have thus wanted to delete it. But it is typical for the Preacher to put thoughts in opposition to each other and to create, as a result of the tension, a feeling of frustration (cf. 1:15, 18; 3:17; 4:10-12, 13; 5:2, 11; etc.). That is what happens here. Labor may be valueless, but it is not totally valueless when compared with laziness. The one pronouncement is true when considered in the light of human envy, and the other pronouncement is true when the relationship between labor and laziness is examined.

The last verse of the poem returns to the idea of the beginning. "Better is a handful of quietness than two hands full of toil" means that small possessions enjoyed in tranquility are to be preferred over large possessions demanding much heavy and useless toil. This statement again reminds the reader of the wisdom of Proverbs (cf. Prov. 17:1, where a dry morsel enjoyed in quietness is viewed as preferable to a table groaning under heavy platters of food in a house where strife prevails), but here again the Preacher's personal purpose is plain: to labor hard is but to strive after wind.

Summary

Two sets of opposing thoughts occur:

Thought:	Labor
Counterthought:	Laziness
Tension:	Relative advantage of labor (but no real advantage)

And

Thought:	Labor
Counterthought:	Envy
Tension:	Vanity of labor

Just as in another place the Preacher throws wholesome cold water over too much trust in one's own value (e.g., 3:16-22), so in this poem he puts a wholesome damper on the ambitions of the workaholic. Envy in particular is examined— a human phenomenon that is all too often accompanied by ambition and by which people harm not only themselves but also others. Ambition, by which people consume themselves and devour others, has the same effect as laziness: it ruins people and therefore it is a chasing after wind. By this statement the Preacher confronts people who have a strong need to assert themselves. But here, as elsewhere, it is not enough to make this admission. More has to be said. Not only does the Preacher warn against labor that is motivated by ambition, but he declares *all* labor to be vain.

The apostle Paul has a different view of labor (see 1 Thess. 4:11; 2 Thess. 3:7ff.). For him labor has a positive meaning because it can be placed at the service of the gospel (1 Thess. 2:9; cf. Acts 18:3). That makes all the difference. Outside of this perspective labor has at best only relative value till it disappears, without a trace, in the wind. But when labor serves that which is permanent, it has permanent value. We do not need to decide between the Preacher and Paul, then. Each, from his own point of view, is right; the important question is on what basis we human beings want to do our work.

THE WORTHLESSNESS OF LABOR (2) 4:7-12

This poem differs from the preceding not only in that it views labor from another perspective but also in that a number of illustrations illuminate the real point. The two strophes that make up the poem have the same structure: the first and last lines of each enclose the lines in between; the declaration of futility occurs in verses 7 and 8d; and in verses 9 and 12b we have a declaration in the form of explicit or implicit "better than" statements saying that the opposite of solitariness is to be preferred.

The first strophe starts in the autobiographical form of a report of what the Preacher has observed. The repeated declaration of futility shows that in his opinion there is an extremely tragic phenomenon: a person is alone, without people around him—without even family, like a brother or a son. In the ancient Eastern world that was an extraordinarily sad state of affairs. But there is more. This individual has done a great amount of hard work and has accumulated great wealth. Now what is the sense of it all? There is no heir to whom the products of his labor can be left; therefore we again encounter the rhetorical question with an implied negative answer—I have toiled in vain. At the beginning of verse 8 the subject was indefinite ("there was a man"), but here in the question in the third line of the same verse the Preacher suddenly uses the first person singular as though he were himself that tragic figure. Some scholars even try to draw conclusions from this concerning the private life of the unknown Preacher, namely, that he must have been alone and secretly pined for the security of a circle of friends and the joys of family life. Such conclusions cannot be made from a poem like this, however. The shift from "a man" to "I" shows instead the strong feelings of the speaker and his intense involvement in the tragedy of what he has seen.

The second strophe starts abruptly with a statement declaring how desirable it is that people do their work communally, for when there is cooperation profit can be expected. The advantage is spelled out in three illustrations. If one falls down a friend can help him up (v. 10). If two lie down together they get warm whereas one who is alone does not (v. 11). The inference that the Preacher was homophile has been drawn from this verse, but this is not supported by either the Hebrew form or the content. It is just a well-established factual proposition that two bodies generate more heat than one. The third illustration says that though one person may be overcome when assaulted, the attacker can be resisted by joint opposition (v. 12a)—in unity there is strength. The poem then ends with a proverb. By beginning the strophe with "two" and ending with "three" the Preacher stresses the opposite of solitariness. So when a person is accompanied by others human enterprise is more likely to succeed. But when a person has to work alone such labor is useless. It seems, then, that we have finally encountered a positive thought in the mind of the Preacher.

What we are dealing with here, however, is only a *seemingly* positive valuation of labor. The presence of the negative judgment at the beginning of the poem, the serious "I" style by which the Preacher enters into the tragic situation of another, the repeated declaration of futility, and the accompaniment of every positive illustration in verses 10-12 by a negative opposite—all these things show unmistakably that the weight of the evidence lies on the side of solitariness, and they all accentuate the worthlessness of labor. This can be seen even more clearly when we look at a diagram of opposing pairs of thought.

Summary

Thought:	Labor
Counterthought:	Community
Result:	Success in labor

The opposing sequence:

Thought:	Labor
Counterthought:	Solitariness
Result:	Futility of labor

But since labor can take place in either community or solitariness, either result may take place. The laborer has no control over whether God will lay loneliness on him or grant him the community of others—that is the uncertain and arbitrary element that may frustrate him as he labors. In other words:

Thought:	Labor
Counterthought:	Absence of control
Tension:	All human labor remains captive to "vanity"

So we cannot say that the Preacher entertains a positive view of human labor. Even success in labor is subject to uncertainty and tension, as is the joy to which the Preacher calls his disciples (e.g., 3:12-13; 11:9-10).

In this poem, as in the preceding one, the Preacher's thoughts on labor are governed by the question of its value— which is not at all surprising because that agrees entirely with the basic question that stands at the very outset of the book: "What does man gain by all the toil at which he toils?" (1:3). His concern is not with the responsibility of man for his labor, still less with the question whether other people benefit from it. That each of them individually draws advantage from cooperation is the only reason why people should join forces when they work. The slogan "In unity there is strength" is viewed only from the standpoint of individual advantage. So in the mind of the Preacher there is no concern to labor out of love for one's neighbor or to labor in service of the community.

We can agree with his rejection of the life of the hermit but not just because the solitary life is not profitable. All labor performed from motives of strictly personal advantage falls outside the luminous circle of Christ's love command and is therefore subject to the uncertainty and emptiness of life. On the other hand, labor motivated by faith in Christ is a service to others mandated by God; such labor is freed from anxiety over whether one's fate will turn out to be favorable or unfavorable.

THE VAGARIES OF POPULAR FAVOR 4:13-16

The first part of this passage consists of a brief story whose purpose is to teach (see also 9:14-15). Repeated attempts have been made to determine who that old king and that young man were. Although numerous proposals have been made to link the data of the poem with corresponding incidents in history, not one of these attempts has been successful. The reason is not hard to find, though; the author is not offering a report but a parable with a message. This is not to say that the Preacher did not make use of remembered material from the past. The story does have echoes of the past in it—of the story of Joseph, to mention a possibility. Although Joseph never became king in the place of Pharaoh, he did leave prison to become a great ruler, and he was wise but later forgotten (Gen. 41:14, 39-40; Exod. 1:8). Since this tradition was known in the circles of the wisdom teachers it is easily possible that the Preacher shaped his own little story under its influence.

He begins here, as elsewhere, with a positive-sounding proverb. Both in form (a "better than" proverb) and in content it fits well in the context of general wisdom. In essence it makes the point that wisdom is better than folly even when there is a huge distinction in class between the wise man and the foolish man. The old king is a classic example of foolishness because, in contrast to wisdom's appreciation for good advice (Prov. 11:14; 15:22; 20:18; 24:6), he pays no attention to the warnings of his advisers. This praise of wisdom is sustained in the remainder of the story.

Despite his initial social disadvantage and his imprisonment, the poor young man assumes the kingship (v. 14). That proves the correctness of the proverb. But we are also given a glimpse of the circumstances that attend the political revolution. The entire population was on the side of the young man (v. 15). The Preacher again (as in 4:1, 4) uses a conscious exaggeration when he says that the entire world population without exception had chosen in favor of the young man. This suggests the general validity of the point he wants to make: such things happen not just occasionally but as a rule. In this verse we are forced to deviate from those versions that translate the text to say that the young man would take the throne by legal succession. The latter part of verse 15 clearly lets the idea of a revolution come through: the masses have chosen in favor of the young man while he was still subject to the king; that is, before the throne was even vacant the masses followed him as their leader, and with their help he became the new king.

Verse 16 puts the story in a more general framework. There is no end to the masses of people who choose in favor of such new leaders. In our view the best possible translation of this verse is one that makes a general point.* Every revolutionary leader is able to convince the masses that they will be better off under him than under their present dictator. In other words, as a rule the ability of the demagogue is such that he can turn popular opinion to his advantage. But then what happens? The later ones no longer applaud his efforts. This may mean that the later subjects of the king will again follow the same route and look for a new advocate to promote their interests, or it may also mean that later generations will have no good reason to recall with gratitude the administration of the young man. In either case the message is that popular favor is fickle. One moment the masses cry "Hosanna"; the next, "Crucify him!" (as one commentator adroitly remarks). Now what use is his wisdom?—none at all; it has become worthless to him. There is no indication in the text that the young man later became a fool and fell out of favor for that reason. If that were the case the passage would serve to prove the value of wisdom: it would then be an example of how one can attain success only with the aid of wisdom. That, however, would be in conflict with the actual text before us and with the general tenor of the book.

Summary

> Thought: Wisdom
> Counterthought: Folly
> Tension: *Relative* advantage of wisdom

And

> Thought: Wisdom
> Counterthought: The vagaries of life
> Tension: The worthlessness of wisdom

The conclusion here is the same as that of the long poem in 1:12–2:26, only here it applies to the political arena. True, wisdom is better than folly because it enabled the intelligent young man to win the favor of the populace and brought him to the throne. But it has no real worth because it does not last. The favor of the masses is fickle; it can turn around like a

---

*The author translates: "There is no end to the crowds for everyone who has become their leader; nevertheless the later ones will not rejoice over them."—Trans.

weathervane and so reduce the value of wisdom to nothing. The real purpose of the poem, however, is not to brood over the unreliability of people in general but to show how that fickleness can just as easily break as make political competence. No one has a firm grip on it—it is too fitful and freakish. Therefore in politics there is room only for pessimism.

One who has Utopian expectations of politics will be disenchanted by the Preacher. Even if there were a revolution by which the status quo changed for the better, no ideal state would come into being. The ideal will never be found here below. When the Preacher presents an unfavorable judgment of political competence, that judgment applies to all political wisdom and leads to general political passivity (cf. 8:2-9). And that in turn would mean that this area of life would come to lie outside the world of faith: the action, responsibilities, and witness of faith would not function meaningfully here. No one who has experienced the claim of Christ upon the totality of his world can agree to this. Granted that the ideal will never be found here below, there is still meaning in political involvement and wisdom.

TALK VERSUS SILENCE 5:1-9

It is hard to tell precisely where this poem ends because it seems that in verses 8 and 9 a new theme is struck. Nonetheless, there is a formal reason why we should link these verses with the poem beginning at 5:1 rather than with the section beginning at 5:10. This next section is written in the narrative style of the third person, whereas the disputed verses (8-9) are in the address style of the second person—exactly like the rest of the poem that precedes them. Upon closer scrutiny, verses 8 and 9 will also prove capable of being linked thematically with the earlier verses.

The structure of the piece is quite regular. In the first part are a number of sections that deal with aspects of human speech in the context of worship; next follows a general statement (v. 7); and in conclusion there are the four difficult lines of verses 8 and 9.

The first point is a warning to be careful about speech in worship. The house of God is the temple where sacrifices are made. The Preacher here points out that it is better to draw near for the purpose of listening than to bring sacrifices like a fool. To "draw near" in the Old Testament often means to approach and participate in a worship service. Listening is the opposite of speaking, and thus in the opinion of the Preacher the best way to participate in worship is to listen in silence. Fools make mistakes when they attend a worship service, and that can result in doing evil. So the Preacher issues his warning. But a warning is not the same as a repudiation. He respects the venerable tradition of worship but obviously has his reservations and keeps his distance. This accords with what we already saw of his God-concept: God is an enormous power before whom people must stand in awe. For that reason it is perilous to take part in the worship of this God, and it is better just to listen quietly than to take part unthinkingly. With that the foundation for the rest of the poem has been laid.

The virtue of listening well and the warning against the dangers of speech form a widespread theme in ancient Eastern wisdom (cf. Prov. 2:1-2; 4:1; 5:1; 17:27-28). While other wisdom teachers mean this as good advice for the one who wishes to manage his life well, its intent for the Preacher is turned around—to cause one to shrink back in fear of this dangerous divine power. What was optimistic for one becomes pessimistic for the other.

The Preacher discusses prayer as the second aspect of speech in worship. "To utter a word before God" (5:2) is to pray. His warning against hasty prayer is obviously not a plea for its abolition—any more than he wants to abolish the ministry of sacrifice. He offers a specific reason why in his view speech directed to God should be rather sparing: "God is in heaven, and you upon earth." This is certainly one of the most telling pronouncements that enlightens our study of the Preacher's God-concept. God is the far off, remote power; there is a gap between him and human beings. It is not possible to bridge it by way of speech. Prayer is not so much wrong as senseless. Considering God's greatness in relation to man's puniness, the Preacher sees no reason why God should bother to listen to prayer. His reasoning is the precise opposite of the usual view of prayer. Whereas people usually pray because they believe that God, by virtue of his greatness, has the power to help them, the Preacher believes that God's power is precisely the reason he cannot be moved by a mere human being to do one thing rather than another. It is noteworthy that the same sort of reasoning occurs in connection with an excess of words in 6:11, where again the topic is the presence of a stronger power (6:10).

In 5:3 the Preacher again supports his argument with a proverb. Just as preoccupation with many cares produces restless dreams, the use of too many words gives prominence to folly. The reference to verboseness refers, of course, to prayers that are too long or too repetitive or too frequent, since in this context prayer is the subject under discussion. The Preacher's point is that too much prayer is folly—precisely the opposite of the point Paul makes in his letter to the Thessalonians when he writes, "Pray without ceasing" (1 Thess. 5:17, KJV). In the abstract the proverb has nothing to do with prayer, of course; it agrees completely with the theme of the relative advantages of silence and speech that recurs in the general wisdom literature of the day (cf. Prov. 10:19). Again the Preacher shows here both his solidarity with established wisdom and his opposition to it: he takes over its ideas but uses them in a manner that changes their meaning into the opposite.

The third illustration of the subject is the making of vows (vv. 4-5). Just as in the previous two situations, the Preacher does not prohibit an action here—the making of a vow—but rather instills a reserved attitude toward it. This view also has echoes in the book of Proverbs (20:25). In Proverbs the emphasis is that one must think before uttering a vow; in Ecclesiastes, that it is better not to utter one at all. Overhastiness in speech is also a form of folly, and God has no pleasure in a fool.

Verse 6 presents yet another specific statement concerning cultic speech and silence: a person's mouth can lead him into sin. If he has said something he later regrets, he must tell the temple messenger that it was a mistake. Because the context deals with worship, the "messenger" has to be someone sent by God—a priest. One who has to confess a mistake to a priest has to appeal to a technical point to get out of it— which can be very embarrassing and rather expensive (see the laws on restitution in Lev. 5:15ff.). Even though the law of Moses considered such unintentional sins forgivable upon payment of a penalty, the Preacher states that God can nevertheless become angry over the words of a thoughtless speaker and this person may have to suffer for it. The Preacher's use of his characteristic rhetorical question indicates that he takes seriously the possibility that God would intervene against the speaker. This contrasts sharply with the earlier suggestion that God would *not* intervene (5:2). But both statements have the same function: to underscore the awesome greatness of God.

In verse 7 the text is awkward; presumably a Hebrew word for "injury" that is almost identical to the word for "vanity" has dropped out in the course of repeated copyings. In that case the original text means that many words lead to injury, a reading that would fit well in the context of the poem. Just as dreams dredge up unwholesome phantasies, so an excess of words produces injury. In any case, warns the Preacher, "stand in awe of God" (NIV). Not that he is here prescribing piety—that would be in conflict with what he has just said about sacrifices, prayers, and vows—but he does say that a person must be cautious before God and adopt a reserved attitude toward him.

Finally, we have verses 8 and 9, in which the theme of human speech and the advantage of silence seemingly does not occur. The immediate message in these verses is fortunately clear enough. The Preacher tells his reader (the same one to whom the preceding verses were addressed) not to be surprised at seeing oppression and injustice in the state. There is an obvious explanation for it. It is to be expected when state officials are in the grip of corruption. When high officials spy on their inferiors to keep the pressure on them and to use them for their own ends, the lower officials in turn will put the screws on the people who are the victims of this corruption. The Preacher mentions it as the most common thing in the world and offers no protest—he is merely describing the hard realities. In such a situation it would be an advantage if the king of the land were subject to the production of the fields, for then help and justice might be expected for the exploited people of that land.

But the context of the poem as a whole shows that this is not the case. So again the picture is devoid of comfort. By linking this brief depiction of social and economic corruption with the theme of dangerous speech and preferable silence, the Preacher indicates that there is no point in protesting against these evil conditions. In that situation the best and safest thing to do is to acquiesce in silence. So the things first said about the subject of speech in a cultic connection apply equally in the domain of social and economic affairs.

Summary

Thought:	Permissible speech
Counterthought:	Preferable silence
Tension:	Peril of God's awesomeness

The subject here, "speech is permissible, silence is preferable," plays an optimistic role in established wisdom circles. But when this optimism is viewed in light of God's awesomeness it is clear that the established teachers of wisdom cannot be followed without question. According to the Preacher, their wisdom takes no account of God's power and so they stand exposed in their own weakness.

The Preacher, however, warns us well against an overly informal and comradely relationship with God. In worship and prayer we need to remember that he is in heaven and we are on earth. But if we stopped at this point we would be evading the question the Preacher puts to us. It is clear that he is not saying, "Pray with reverence." Perhaps the effect on his readers will be that they arrive at that insight, but he himself goes further and counsels against speaking with God at all. The apostle Paul, however, does the opposite; he advises us never to stop praying. The God of the Preacher is remote—that comes through more clearly here than anywhere else. Between God and man there is a terrible emptiness; and so only his awesome power becomes visible. But precisely because there is this terrible distance and estrangement it has become necessary to fill the emptiness with a mediator. Since this is the role Christ assumed, he has become the mediator of our prayers. Whoever prays in his name will receive (John 14:13); through him there is access to God for all who are far away, even as far as the Preacher is (Eph. 2:17-18). Therefore we also can pray for help in the difficulties of every day, even when they seem as insurmountable as the Preacher paints them. And it would be wrong now to resignedly accept exploitation and injustice and not to appear before God as advocates of the oppressed and disenfranchised. For he is the supreme sovereign and holder of power as well as the God of justice (Deut. 1:17).

THE WORTHLESSNESS OF RICHES 5:10–6:9

In the interval between two poems about speech and silence (5:1-9 and 6:10-12) there is a long series of eleven reflections on the subject of riches. Three of them take up several lines, but the others are very short—some only a combination of two lines (couplets). We ran into the subject of riches already in 2:1-11, but there the function of the reflection differed radically from what the Preacher asserts here. There riches constituted part of an experiment with folly, but here they are weighed on their own merits. The two lines of verse 10 reinforce each other because they run parallel. Money and riches are marked by the fact that they never satisfy. There is not a lover of money who ever says that he has enough of it. As becomes apparent in verses 18-20, money by itself has a positive value, but that value is immediately relativized by the fact that it enslaves its owner. So when the value of money is measured against the avarice that it occasions, the only conclusion is that money is worthless. For that reason the couplet is concluded by the characteristic declaration of futility: "this also is vanity."

Summary

Thought:	Money (riches)
Counterthought:	Avarice
Tension:	Worthlessness of riches

In verse 11 the second counterpole is posed over against riches. When wealth comes, its consumers inevitably come with it, and their number increases in proportion to the increase of possessions.

The Preacher does not specify whom he has in mind; the consumers of wealth may be relatives and friends—of whom the wealthy have many—but the text may also refer to the personnel or business relations of the rich man. Whoever they may be, the point under discussion is the fact that wealth brings its own consumers along with it. This is what brings about the worthlessness of wealth. In a bitterly ironic rhetorical question in the second line of the verse, the Preacher puts it like this: the man of capital gets no benefit from his riches except to feast his eyes on them!

Summary

Thought:	Possessions
Counterthought:	Consumers
Tension:	Worthlessness

The third couplet (v. 12) contains the third argument against riches. This time the two lines of the verse stand in an antithetical relationship to each other. In the first we hear of a laborer; in the second, of a rich man. The laborer sleeps soundly; the rich man does not sleep at all. A person who has exerted himself physically in the fulfillment of his daily task can sleep well as a rule whether he has eaten a light or a heavy meal. But what is true of the laborer is not true of the rich man. His satiety does not let him sleep. This may mean that he has overindulged himself at his dinner table and is sick as a result or that he lacks wholesome exercise such as the laborer gets or that his surfeit of possessions produces anxiety that makes him unable to sleep. These three possibilities do not, of course, exclude each other, but the comparison between the rich man and the laborer indicates that especially the first two are plausible.

In the wisdom literature of the Sumerians there is a proverb that shows a strong resemblance to our verse: "He who eats too much will not be able to sleep." It is meant as a warning against eating too much, hence as a piece of good advice. But the Preacher uses the idea for his own purpose, namely, to show that wealth is worthless—if it causes sleeplessness it cannot be very valuable. So again he adopts an idea in general circulation but uses it with a different intent from that of the teachers of wisdom.

Summary

Thought:	Riches
Counterthought:	Sleeplessness
Tension:	Worthlessness

The author devotes a quatrain to the following observation (vv. 13-14). To the Preacher it applies to a grievous misfortune he has had to deal with in his life. From his intense language some interpreters have concluded that he was somehow personally involved in the case. This is unlikely, however, because he speaks only of what he has observed, not of what he has experienced. When mention is made here of riches that have been hoarded to the harm of the owner, it sounds as if riches themselves bring ruin. In light of the following lines (v. 14a), however, this is likely not the case. The wealth was lost through some misfortune (perhaps fire, theft, or a human mistake) and that means that all the labor and toil spent on gathering and taking care of it was in vain. The disadvantage, then, was that all this care was costly to the owner but did not profit him in the end. If the man had a son, he has no inheritance to leave him. Then what value do all these riches have for him? It is important for us to note carefully the assumption underlying this reflection. If the disadvantage of the accumulation of riches does not arise until they are lost, that means the riches by themselves can be valuable indeed. So we are again dealing with the relative value of things. In some circumstances riches may have value, but in other circumstances the value disappears. That will become clear in verses 18-20. The tension lies in that man is a helpless and vulnerable being in a world where accidents happen without warning and can wipe out in seconds what has taken years to build up. Because these happenstances lie outside one's control, and because the usefulness of riches is subject to them, riches are unreliable.

Summary

Thought: Riches
Counterthought: Misfortune
Tension: Worthlessness

In verses 15 and 16 a quatrain follows that contains a fifth way of looking at the worthlessness of riches. With regard to possessions, the day of a man's death and the day of his birth are the same—he enters life without possessions and leaves it without possessions. The remark that a man returns in the way he came from his mother's womb does not mean he returns to his mother's womb; it is just an expression describing the similarity between a man's condition at birth and his condition at death (this also applies to Job 1:21 where Job, too, says that he will return). So we do not need to repeat the misunderstanding of Nicodemus that occurred when Jesus spoke of the second birth (John 3:4). According to the Preacher, the tragedy is that all the toil that goes into the accumulation of riches does not produce anything that will still be useful after death. The concluding words of verse 15 concern not the disadvantaged heir whose misfortune was discussed in the previous pericope (v. 14) but the owner himself. That is the well-known wisdom of everyman, which says that no one can take his possessions into death with him. "There are no pockets in a shroud." So if death overrules riches, the effort with which they were gathered is, of course, futile. The worthlessness of wealth, therefore, shows up in this case from the counterpole death.

Summary

Thought:	Riches
Counterthought:	Death
Tension:	Worthlessness

The sixth phenomenon by which wealth is deprived of its glamor and lustre is mentioned in verse 17. The rich man has to eat his food in darkness. One must not take this statement literally as though the rich man ate in an unlighted workroom because in his greed he did not allow himself time or space for a proper meal. In keeping with the last part of this verse the darkness must be understood rather as a figure for unfavorable circumstances. The statement then means that the benefits accruing from wealth are spoiled by the attendant difficulties. Vexation or anxiety inevitably comes with great possessions; mental anguish or physical illness is to be expected in view of the responsibilities of the rich man; and resentment easily arises from the tensions that burden him. If he is to possess his wealth under such circumstances, it is hard to see what pleasure remains in it for him. So the Preacher arrives at the same pessimistic conclusion as before:

Thought:	Riches
Counterthought:	Difficulties
Tension:	Worthlessness

Viewed superficially, verses 18-20 strike a very different note. All of a sudden the positive advantages of riches are brought out. For this reason some commentators believe this passage to be a later addition inserted by a conservative editor. But as in all other instances in which such opinions are aired, it is the Preacher himself, and not a later editor, who is saying these things. We again note his characteristic predilection for contrasts. After treating six distinct aspects of the uselessness of riches, he now switches to the opposite. He again reports what he has observed—only he does not invite his readers to enjoyment and pleasure. This is not his usual conclusion in which he advises people only to seek a maximum of pleasure in a bad situation. He does say that he thinks it wonderful whenever a person can celebrate his feasts and enjoy the good things of life after working hard for them. His life, the days of which are his by divine arrangement, is a gift from God, as is the pleasure he experienced in the course of it.

This idea fits the views of the Preacher well, and so we need not drag in the supposed efforts of a conservative editor (cf. 3:12-13). That God is the giver of riches, and that it is he who enables a person to enjoy them (v. 19), implies at the same time that he can also dispose things otherwise. For when such a positive view of wealth is inserted amid so many statements with a negative import, we are forced to note that everything depends on the counterpole that is linked with riches. If it is the possibility of enjoying them, then good. If it is unfortunate circumstances of which we have heard earlier, then wealth is worthless. But who is responsible for the apportionment of favorable and unfavorable circumstances? God is—and his work is unpredictable and hence uncertain. By hinting at this unreliability and at the consequent lack of certainty for man, the Preacher draws even the favorable aspect of riches into the atmosphere of his pessimism.

Summary

Thought:	Riches
Counterthought:	Pleasure
Result:	Opposite of worthlessness

But the result is contingent on the uncertain apportionment by God and so is no less subject to tension than the other instances.

Precisely the opposite point is expressed in 6:1-2. Sometimes God gives a person everything that is desirable to man: extensive possessions, much money, and standing in the community (a very understandable addition, for a person with money as a rule carries weight in society whether it is morally deserved or not). But then he creates another counterpole that obviously renders all these things worthless. It may be impossible for this man of wealth and status to enjoy them. The Preacher does not say precisely what these negative circumstances are because they may assume a variety of forms. The rich man may be sickly or may be a schizophrenic who is not well balanced in his judgment; or his children may cause him sorrow. Numerous things could be cited that show that God does not always enable the man of wealth to enjoy his riches. In such a situation someone else is the beneficiary of his riches. Not the heir but a stranger—a nonrelative or even a member of another nation. So the rich man does not even have the satisfaction that his own descendant will enjoy the fruits of his possessions. That is an evil that weighs heavily on men—not only because the rich man suffers but also because it poses a painful question: Why should God give this man these gifts in the first place if he does not intend him to enjoy their benefits? For the Preacher this is an essentially unanswerable question because no one knows what God is doing (cf. 3:11). This again makes evident the enormous distance between the remote ruler in heaven and helpless man on earth. Hence the conclusion, a double statement of futility: "vanity" and "a sore affliction."

Summary

Thought:	Riches
Counterthought:	No enjoyment
Tension:	Worthlessness

The Preacher becomes even more severe in verses 3-6. He now opposes the two conflicting thoughts at length. Suppose a man has a hundred children, he says. He can then be regarded as especially blessed because children are viewed as a good gift of God (see Ps. 127:3). And suppose he lives to a ripe old age; then he is especially privileged, for a long life is also considered a gift from God (see Prov. 16:31). But what if for some reason he cannot enjoy his prosperity during all those years, and what if he gets no proper burial? That, then, is a special misfortune (cf. 2 Kings 9:33ff.; Isa. 14:19; etc.), especially since not one of his hundred children will make the effort to accord their final respects to their dead father. Just how bad that is comes out in the Preacher's strongly worded judgment: a stillborn child is better off than he. That is about the harshest conceivable judgment one can make (cf. 4:3). Stillborn children come and go in darkness, total nonparticipants in the drama of life. They have no name or identity. They never see the sun. In other words, they experience none of the vicissitudes of human life. For that reason a stillborn child is better off than the rich man: such a child at least has peace.

In verse 6 the author briefly summarizes the case to underscore his profound conviction. Even if the rich man's long life doubles the world record (achieved by Methuselah, who lived 969 years—Gen. 5:27), it remains of no value because there was no chance to enjoy it. The conclusion is a rhetorical question in which the author asserts that all go to the same place—that is, to the domain of spectres in the underworld. To say that the stillborn child and the rich man have the same destination is a very bitter way of underscoring that the former has the advantage simply because he never had to experience the burdens and cares of life. It means further that the tragedy of life, and not the blessings of life, increases with the passing of the years. Thus the so-called blessings are actually a curse in certain circumstances.

Summary

Thought:	A life surrounded by the traditional blessings
Counterthought:	No enjoyment from it; death
Tension:	Worthlessness—even injury from material "blessings"

In verses 7 and 8 the Preacher combines the subject of possessions with that of wisdom. All man's efforts are for his mouth—that is, people labor to make an income that can be used to buy food. Thus, according to the Preacher, all labor ultimately has to do with the production of food. But over against this mass of food that man makes for himself stands a counterpole: the appetite for food never stops making demands. Real satisfaction never does take place, for a human being always wants to eat again. The human mouth is the opening to a bottomless pit that can never be filled. Viewed from this perspective, possessions seem worthless because they serve a senseless goal.

At the same time this view offers the author another opportunity to attack established wisdom. The rhetorical question with which verse 8 begins posits that the wise man has no advantage over the fool. In the course of his grand experiment with wisdom and folly described in 1:12ff., the Preacher determined that the wise man did have an advantage over the fool but that this advantage was only relative. Now we learn how insignificant such an advantage really is: it is so small that one could say it is no *real* advantage at all. Wisdom and skill are necessary to produce foodstuffs, but the possible usefulness of food (filling the ever hungry mouth) is so meaningless that the source of it (wisdom) is also questionable and hence of no greater value than senseless folly.

Parallel to this pronouncement on wisdom stands the second line of verse 8. The Hebrew consonants of one word appear to have been changed around erroneously by a copyist so that it seems the text speaks of a poor man (see KJV, RSV, NIV). But that does not make sense in this connection. What could it mean that the poor man is contrasted with someone who knows how to conduct himself in life or that the poor man has no advantage over such a person? The best reading is probably that the Preacher refers to himself here, asking why he is making all this effort to find out how he must conduct himself in life. That would be reminiscent of his experiment with wisdom (1:12ff.) and would underscore that the relative value of that wisdom is also of no real value.

Summary

Thought:	Labor for an income
Counterthought:	Insatiability
Tension:	Worthlessness of income

And

Thought:	Wisdom
Counterthought:	Folly
Tension:	Worthlessness

Finally, in verse 9, the Preacher again brings up the thought of death. The expression translated as "the roving of the appetite" (NIV) or "the wandering of desire" (RSV) must instead be understood as referring to dying. The same Hebrew word is used three times in this passage for "departing" or "dying" (5:15, 16; 6:4) and most likely has that meaning here as well. "What the eye sees" (NIV) denotes the actual pleasure a person takes in a given reality. This is in agreement with 5:18-20, where it was shown to be possible for a person to enjoy the fruits of his possessions. Here the Preacher is concerned that no one be overly optimistic about the prospect, because sooner or later pleasure is confronted by that inevitable counterpole: death! Then what is left of pleasure? A double declaration of futility follows: it is vanity and striving after wind. Pleasure is preferable to death, but no one escapes that fate. So this, too, is an appropriate final link in the chain of antithetical statements.

Summary

Thought:	Enjoyment of possessions
Counterthought:	Death
Tension:	Emptiness

This series of reflections can be read in different ways. One may find in them a good moral lesson concerning the incompleteness and vanity of wealth. This notion is not itself wrong, since no one can deny that the Preacher has said appalling words about the worthlessness of wealth. Wisdom literature in general is full of warnings against a materialistic mind-set (cf. Prov. 8:19; 11:28; Ps. 49:16-20), but for the Preacher the function of these warnings is different from that of the wisdom writers' sayings. They offer wise advice for the successful conduct of life; he exposes the emptiness of all aspects of life. Again we see, as so often in this volume, how the Preacher takes over an idea from wisdom literature but uses it in a way that makes it say the very opposite. His little lesson on the error of materialism is therefore in no way the last word intended in the passage.

But is the Preacher's view of money and possessions complete? Is it true that these things can be judged only negatively? The Preacher views material prosperity only from an egocentric point of view; in his thinking only the aspect of personal consumption and pleasure plays a role. But material well-being can also be focused on one's neighbor and can be a means of service.

When material goods are no longer the all-consuming goal of life, then riches need no longer be a manifestation of the complete emptiness of life. There is another perspective than that of the Preacher. If it is possible to look foward to conditions in heaven, then conditions on earth do not lose their value but instead gain meaning when others can be served with them (Mark 10:21). For that reason those who look forward to a future that the Preacher could not yet see cannot relate as passively as he does to earthly things (cf. 4:1-3). They cannot say to the poor: "Go in peace, be warmed and filled" without also giving them "the things needed for the body" (James 2:16). A vision different from that of the Preacher is needed if we are to be compassionately concerned about the collective well-being of mankind and the exercise of mercy among ourselves (1 Cor. 16:1-3) as well as the progress of the gospel (Rom. 15:24).

And his repeated assertion that God is responsible for all wealth as well as the enjoyment or lack of enjoyment of wealth—is that the whole story? Does that not cause huge problems for us? If material possessions are a gift from God and at the same time completely meaningless, then God's gifts are vain and worthless.

Does God play games with us? According to the Preacher he does (6:1-2): he can set the whole stage for the enjoyment of riches and then hold back; he can set the banquet table and forbid the guests to eat. In light of the new perspective Christ has brought into our lives, the views of the Preacher, possible only in his own day, must be reinterpreted. Not all material well-being is God's gift.

The riches of a swindler and the prosperity of an exploitative society are not gifts from God but something they have appropriated for themselves. The poverty of the exploited and the suffering of the children of the oppressed are not the consequences of God's witholding the means of enjoyment but are the responsibility of the exploiters. God has no part in the exploits of sin, though he can use and overrule it in the context of redemption.

WORDS OF THE POWERLESS 6:10-12

Both the idea of human powerlessness and the idea of human speech occur in this short poem. Again we note the structural framework: at the center is the statement on the effect of words (v. 11), and surrounding it on both sides are utterances concerning human impotence (vv. 10 and 12). Similar patterns occur in 3:10-15, 16-22, and 10:2-7. Because speech plays a role in this poem, there is a measure of symmetry in the arrangement of the poems of this book: in 5:1-9 the subject is human speech, in 5:10–6:9 it is wealth, and here in 6:10-12 it is speech again.

The first words of the poem make an abrupt break with the preceding passage. The subject here is the predestination of all that exists; the existence of all things that have come into being is determined in advance. In the conceptual world of the time there was a very close connection between creation and the giving of names (see Gen. 1:6, 8, 10; Ps. 147:4; Isa. 40:26). That connection is present here too, so we must regard the naming of things as the determination of their nature. Although the Preacher does not expressly say that it is God who is the predeterminer, this is clearly his intention. It was customary at that time to refer to God in a concealed way by using the passive form of the verb—something the Preacher does twice in the same line. Also the "one stronger," against whom man cannot fight, has to be a reference to God. Since all things have been determined by God, man's essence was fixed by God from before the creation. If man lies so completely in the hand of God that without his will he cannot so much as move (see the Heidelberg Catechism, Lord's Day 10), it follows that man cannot fight God. This is not to deny that man can fancy himself capable of such a struggle and will make a fruitless effort in that direction. Job made that mistake: despite his initial acknowledgment that no one is able to persevere (Job 9:2-3), he nevertheless tried (consider the outcome, Job 40:3-5). The quarrel the author has in mind here is a legal contest between God and man. Considered superficially this statement can be construed as being very pious. It could mean that a human being ought not rebel against God's righteousness. But in the context of this book that cannot be the intent. God is pictured here as the overwhelmingly superior One, and man as a powerless mite. In such an unequal relationship man is totally dependent on God and lacks the capacity to present his case. What the Preacher says here, with more than a trace of bitterness, is that might makes right.

To this statement is linked the middle verse (11), which deals with human words. In light of his impotence and in the face of God's superiority man had best keep silent. His words are meaningless anyway, and the meaninglessness increases in proportion to the number of words used. A person can win no battle with a multitude of words—as Job tried—especially when the adversary is also the judge. There is no profit, then, in rebellious words.

Verse 12 adds a second consideration to that of verse 10 concerning man's extreme limitations, namely, his ignorance. The rhetorical question with which the verse begins expressly says that no one knows what is good for man. His lifespan is short, his knowledge limited. No one can tell him what will happen on earth after he is gone. At this point the Preacher shows both how profoundly he differs from the prophets whose entire purpose it was to make known God's will for the present and the future and also how his book differs from apocalyptic literature, the purpose of which was to make known what will happen in the future. This, then, is all the more reason why a person should keep his mouth shut; the talk of one who is ignorant serves no good purpose.

So talk and silence stand as opposites to each other; in between them is the tension of God's superior power over man the midget. As we have seen, the comparison of speech and silence is a favorite topic in wisdom literature, one on which it offers its usual optimistic advice. But the Preacher uses it in his usual pessimistic manner, so that it turns into criticism of established wisdom.

Summary

Thought:	Speech
Counterthought:	Silence
Tension:	God's superior power over man, the insignificant creature;

And

Thought:	Typical wisdom topic
Counterthought:	God's superior power over insignificant man
Tension:	Rejection of prevailing wisdom

Although the subject of the poem is the topic of speech versus silence, the really fascinating component is the context in which it occurs. Speech is useless because man is a being in the hands of God. This implies that the Preacher's concept of God's foreordination is extremely negative, while in the rest of the Old Testament foreordination is presented positively. Election by God is usually viewed as a goal-oriented predetermination of the destiny of man. A good example of this election can be found in Deuteronomy 7:6ff., which clearly shows that God's election of the people of Israel was inbued with purpose and aimed through time at the destination he had made known to their fathers long before. But the Preacher says that no man knows what will happen in the future. Again, that is not the speech of ordinary piety; it excludes the elements of promise, certainty, and orientation to the future. It is not enough, therefore, in considering this poem, simply to give pious assent to what the Preacher says, namely, that we do not know what the future holds. The fact is that he sweeps all certainties aside. This is logical, for people cannot have any certainties if they cannot picture a destiny for themselves; and they can see no destiny if God does not show them one. Therefore, God has, in his love, established a final goal and destiny for all and sent them on their way (Deut. 7:8).

If since the time of Ecclesiastes our view of the future has changed so much, then our view of God's power of predetermination also changes. Of course, no one can enter into judgment with God. Job discovered that. But now we can turn to God, knowing his might does not exclude his love. For that reason we cannot be content to view God's power as blind caprice against which we have no defense and by which we feel we have been done an injustice. A theologian has described God as the "defenseless superiority," and it is true that God allows the interests, the actions, and the words of human beings to affect and move him. When this happens, God uses his superior power to man's advantage, because he does not wish to enter into judgment with him.

DEATH IS BETTER THAN LIFE 7:1-4

This series of proverbial sayings presupposes the question, "What is good for man?" For that reason three out of four have been fittingly cast into the form of the "better than" proverb that occurs frequently in wisdom literature (e.g., Prov. 3:14; 8:11; 15:16-17; etc.). The Preacher thus uses a current form to express his thoughts, but his content, too, was currently a subject of interest to wisdom in general—namely, the question of what is good for man. The manner in which he deals with it, however, is peculiarly his own, as will soon be evident. It is possible that the poem was placed here because verse 12 of the preceding passage asked the question what is good for man in life while from verse 5 on a number of "better than" sayings follow.

The first proverb (v. 1) consists of two parallel parts and states expressly that death is better than life. When the Preacher says that the day of death is better than the day of birth, he means he prefers the one over the other. He has expressed this preference before (4:2), but in other places he says the opposite (e.g., in 9:4, where, however, the implication is still as pessimistic as it is in the other passages). The first half of the verse makes the same point about death and life. In Hebrew a name sometimes signifies the fame of a person who has died (e.g., Prov. 10:7; Job 18:17), while ointment or oil is a metaphor for life (derived from the idea of the lamp of life which burns oil—see Prov. 13:9; 20:20). For the Preacher himself there is no such thing as remembered fame after death (see 1:11; 2:16); here he uses the general idea only in order to refer to death itself. So the first half of the verse says in a graphic way that death is to be preferred over life. The implication is that nothing essentially good happens in life. Because the Preacher has no hopes for a life after death, he thinks man basically has nothing good to live for. The advantage of death is that the dead have no share in the toil and chasing after wind that takes place during life.

Verse 2 contains two lines, the second giving the motivation for the Preacher's viewpoint. A house of mourning is a house in which people perform the rituals of mourning because a death has entered it. This is clear from the second line, in which the author refers to death as the destiny of every person. Over against the house where death has made its appearance there is the house of feasting. Present here is the counterpole of death—vitality. The point is not that the author prefers sadness to joy but that he prefers that which underlies the sadness of those who mourn. Going to the house of mourning is "useful"—not because the mourners are comforted by the condolences of the visitors but because the living are confronted with the fact that death is also their own destiny. The only thing that is certain is death. Precisely the same idea occurs in a different way in 9:4-5, where the ironic statement is made that life is better than death because the living know they will die and the dead know nothing.

Preference for sorrow over joy is also expressed in verse 3 but in more general terms. Sorrow is more inclusive than grief occasioned by a death, and laughter is not limited to houses of feasting. By this statement the Preacher expands the sphere of human sadness, as it were, so that it is established as something that is generally to be preferred over joy. For that reason he makes the statement that the signs of sorrow on a person's face show that in his heart all is well. In the context this state of "wellness" is only relative, however, and not real.

The last verse again refers to the house of mourning as contrasted with the house of pleasure and hence carries the same idea as verse 2. This time, however, the thought is added that wise men have their heart in the atmosphere of sadness, and fools in the atmosphere of pleasure. Since the preceding verses show that the first deserves preference, the obvious implication is a preference for wisdom over folly. By this combination of preferences the Preacher launches another of his sharp attacks on the wisdom teachers of his day. Both the praise of wisdom and the idea of the wholesome effects of sorrow (not to mention the "better than" form of the proverbs in verses 1-3) are characteristic of wisdom literature (cf. Prov. 3:11-12; 12:1; Job 33; and the extracanonical Sirach 2:5 and Wisdom 3:5).

Again the Preacher uses accepted ideas with a brand new twist: the wise man has no real advantage except the "advantage" of knowing that death rules over all.

Summary

Thought:	Life
Counterthought:	Death
Tension:	Preponderance of death; meaninglessness

And

Thought:	Accepted wisdom that grief is wholesome
Counterthought:	The Preacher's view that all things are meaningless
Tension:	Worthlessness of accepted wisdom

The logical consequence of the conviction expressed here, according to some, would be an escape by suicide. The Preacher is held back from this radical kind of consistency, however, by his own conclusion that a person should enjoy whatever opportunity for enjoyment comes his way (see 3:12-13, 22; 8:15; 9:7-10). Furthermore, in his view death is not better than life in the sense that it provides a meaningful escape from a hard world but "better" only in the sense that it strikes the dominant note in life. For that reason it is a "good" thing to take serious account of it.

If we at all costs wish to hear nothing but edifying words from the Preacher, we shall have to apply the techniques of international diplomacy and close our eyes to the real contents of what he says, noting only an occasional facet. We could then say that he in fact offers good advice, for sooner or later everyone has to deal with his own death. But he does not leave it to us to make out what precisely is entailed in death. He says expressly that death is the end of every man—the last, triumphant enemy. That is to say, man is helpless and powerless in the face of the unstoppable destruction of death. This awesome statement is undeniably true. If it were not, man himself would be able to overcome death and would not have needed help. But a helper has come who has unseated this last enemy from its throne (1 Cor. 15:26). Without this helper it is indeed better to go into a house of mourning and to stay there.

THE FRUSTRATION OF WISDOM 7:5-7

The first line of this brief reflection is a "better than" saying, which makes it understandable why this fragment was placed between the preceding proverbs and the following two reflections (all of which make use of a "better than" proverb). Still, this is a separate poem whose theme differs from the preceding (life and death) as well as from the following (speech and silence).

Again a word in praise of wisdom! The virtue of wise action as opposed to the vice of foolishness (v. 5) is an undeniable emphasis of wisdom literature in general (cf. Prov. 21:22; 24:5). The Preacher picks a more subtle, or less naive, proverb to link up his statement with the idea of the preceding poem that there is something wholesome in the unpleasant. The value of wisdom lies in the unpleasant rebuke of a wise man (cf. Prov. 12:1; 15:10). On the other hand, although it is pleasant to listen to the praise of people whose judgment is worthless, what is the point? It is clear that wisdom wins hands down when contrasted with folly.

In verse 6 the Preacher underscores this view with still another proverb, this time one that has the form of a comparison. The worthlessness of folly is strongly stressed in a statement that implies an emphatic preference for the wisdom of which the previous verse spoke. Verses 5 and 6 are linked together by the conjunction *for* (RSV), which insures that in verse 6 we shall get to hear the reason why the rebuke of a wise man is preferable to the praise of a fool. The Preacher here employs a number of subtle suggestions to get his idea across. The word for "crackling" can also be used to describe the human voice. Thus the sound of foolish laughter "crackles" like the burning branches of a thornbush. When these thornbushes are first set on fire, moreover, the flames rise quickly and high, but they consume the bush in seconds into a thin layer of ashes and then die out. Beyond that the Preacher plays with the sound of words to bring his proverb to the attention of his readers. The words for "thorns" and "pot" sound identical (*sîr*), and these again sound almost like the word for song in the previous verse (*shîr*). By these techniques the Preacher suggests that the song and the laughter of fools is nothing more than the crackling of burning thornbushes and that the praises and laughter of fools accomplish as little as a flame that does not last long enough to make a pot boil and leaves only some warm ashes. The Preacher finally imitates the sound of sizzling ashes by using words in which these sibilant sounds occur, something the English translation cannot convey. The reason why foolish praise and foolish pleasure are not worth anything, then, is that they have neither duration nor effect. So in his own ingenious way the Preacher makes exactly the same point about wisdom and folly that he made before.

But is wisdom then all that praiseworthy? As always, the Preacher now crushes every possibility of interpreting his words in a positive sense. The last words of verse 6 do not in fact form a conclusion to the previous words. He does not say that foolish laughter and foolish praise are meaningless; he has already done that with great ingenuity in the sound- and wordplays of the preceding verses. So then the declaration of futility serves as an introduction to the following verse.

Verse 7 should not begin with "surely" (RSV). The lines that follow are statements of possibilities—things that are very well conceivable but that do not necessarily have to take place. It is very well possible, for instance, that a wise man can be made into a fool by extortion. The oppressive influence of any given power can subvert, in subtle and unnoticed ways, the perspective and intelligent integrity of wise people. The second half of verse 7 shows even more clearly what the author means because the case is pictured more concretely. Here the reference is to a bribe that can corrupt the human heart. To the ancient man of the East the heart was the organ of thought. Balanced judgment and true wisdom can be adversely affected by the gain the wise man is offered. He who pays the piper calls the tune. The Preacher does not say that all wise men do fall prey to such unjust pressure and so become fools; he only points out what may happen. This uncertainty is typical for the Preacher's way of thinking. Nothing is certain and knowable—except death. His statements do show that for him there ought to be no confidence in wisdom. In the first part of the poem accepted wisdom comes off looking good only because its counterpole is folly; but in the last part it comes off badly because it is viewed against the counterpole of the pressures of life (here it is improper pressure).

Summary

> Thought: Wisdom
> Counterthought: Folly
> Tension: Relative advantage of wisdom

And

> Thought: Wisdom
> Counterthought: Pressures of life
> Tension: Worthlessness of wisdom

As is so often done with the words of the Preacher this reflection, too, can be presented to today's reader as being pious and morally positive. But to achieve this effect people have to read these words superficially, going by their sound only and ignoring the cutting way they function in the Preacher's scheme.

We could say, for instance, that it is a piece of universal wisdom to prefer the wholesome effect of a rebuke to hollow and empty praise. We could add that all people need to be warned against corruption, whether bluntly or in a more subtle way. That is very good advice. The church must certainly learn to recognize that genuine and sincere criticism is of much greater value than mutual flattery and that there is a very real danger that people of integrity are being subtly manipulated. But these things we learn from other sources; they are not what the Preacher is about. He only describes what he sees and offers no prescriptions. He only points out the worthlessness of wisdom despite the relative value it has in comparison with folly. To him, the vicissitudes of life also play their destructive role in the sphere of supposed integrity.

Again we have to state that we cannot take this opinion ill of him—is it not realistic and on target? This human tendency has not improved in the world in which we live. But in another respect our world has changed. Christ has come with his impossible demand: "You, therefore, must be perfect, as your heavenly Father is perfect" (Matt. 5:48). Whereas for the Preacher there was no point in doing anything about the teaching of wisdom, and he could matter-of-factly call it vanity, Christians will simply have to attempt the impossible. They will have to distance themselves from spiritual paralysis, rise against it, and never surrender to it. They must hold on to their independence and the freedom to which Christ has called them—even when subtle pressures and large temptations make it easy for them to justify themselves. For they are called to be what they must become—perfect. Christian responsibility demands wisdom, reflection, consultation, planning, self-criticism and the critical evaluation of others. For these reasons wisdom is good in itself, not merely by comparison with folly. It has been made meaningful by its service to Christ.

TO STOP SPEAKING IS BETTER THAN TO START 7:8-10

This is the third poem about the value of speech (cf. 5:1-9 and 6:10-12). The poem begins with two "better than" proverbs in the first line (similar to 7:1, though in the Hebrew the word for "better" occurs only once in 7:1). At the outset, then, we can tell from the form that the Preacher again uses current ways of fashioning proverbial wisdom.

In content also there is similarity with wisdom in general, for the subject is the well-known topic of human speech, a topic to which the wisdom teachers always paid much attention (see the exposition of 4:17). The Hebrew term translated as "thing" in the KJV and the RSV and as "matter" in the NIV should in fact be translated as "word." Although the Hebrew has only one term for both meanings, it is clear from the two parallel halves of verse 8, from the idea of being easily offended in verse 9, and especially from the express mention of speech in verse 10 that the subject is words. But what does it mean, then, that the end of a word is better than its beginning? The author does not say that a word—that is, human speech—is wrong, just that it is undesirable. It is better to stop speaking and to keep quiet than to begin speaking and so break the silence.

This fits well with the parallel half of the verse, though a casual reading may not reveal this. Parallel to one who stops speaking is the patient person, and parallel to one who starts speaking is the proud person. So we are dealing here with a patient silent person as contrasted with a proud vocal person. This can relate equally well to a political situation (as in 8:2-9) and to a cultic situation (as in 5:1-9). If the reference were political, the Preacher would be expressing his disapproval of revolutionary talk and would be advising the reader to accept the status quo. If the reference were to a cultic situation, the author would be expressing his disapproval of one who is so proud that in his prayers he takes no account of the distance between God and man, which for the Preacher is a good reason to be restrained in speech (5:2). Although these possibilities exist we must take this pronouncement rather as a general statement of principle, for in the following two verses the author offers more specific examples to illustrate why silence is better than speech.

In verse 9 the Preacher offers a typical piece of wisdom advising calm in place of annoyance (cf. Prov. 17:27; also 15:1; 25:15). This clearly relates to the patience mentioned in the previous verse. The Preacher opposes "temper"—the spirit of being easily provoked—as a sign of folly. Anger produces words and a loss of self-control. That is the first specific illustration of "untimeliness in speech."

The second illustration (v. 10) also comes in the form of negative advice—the advice to avoid words in which present conditions are compared with those in earlier times. Such statements always label "the good old days" as better than the present. According to the Preacher it is unwise, even foolish, to ask why things used to be better.

Why is such talk foolish? In the first place, the point of view to which the author refers presupposes a doctrine of devolution. Those who so easily assume that the old days were always "good" believe they see a line of descent in life: things always get worse. But the Preacher has concluded from his observations that everything remains the same—past, present, and future are all alike (see 1:9 and 3:15). So the assumption underlying the "good old days" point of view is foolishness. In the second place, the question "Why . . ." in verse 10 is priggish because it makes no sense. God alone determines what will take place, according to the Preacher, and man cannot under any circumstances find out what lies behind the events (see 3:11). For that reason no answer can be given to the question why things are as they are. So it is better to be silent on that subject. In the third place, the question presupposes criticism of the status quo. That, too, had best be left unspoken, for criticism can be dangerous (see 10:20).

This poem is cast in the form of statements of advice. So on the surface it seems that the Preacher follows the practice of general wisdom and merely instructs his disciples in the art of living. But in fact the reverse is the case. He may use the characteristic form of the "better than" proverb and strike the ever-current theme of the wisdom of silence and self-control, but both form and theme function for him in keeping with the pessimistic tenor of the entire book. We have to conclude, therefore, that the Preacher's opposition to the generally optimistic teachers of wisdom never relaxes. According to them when speech and silence are opposing options, silence is to be preferred because it is the more likely to produce success in life. But when the Preacher faces these two poles he prefers silence only because speech is meaningless and restraint is therefore better in comparison.

Summary

Thought:	Speech
Counterthought:	Silence
Tension:	Preference for silence over meaningless speech

If there is one single book in the Bible in which the reader must be alert not only to the denotation of the words but especially to their function in context, it is this collection of poems of the Preacher. How easy it is to reduce these poignant utterances concerning the error of angry speech and priggish questions merely to little moral lessons! Of course, it is all to our advantage to choose our words carefully in self-restraint and not to speak when we are furious; and naturally it is best to avoid senseless questions and not to pine nostalgically for the good old days. But then we must realize that we have not yet fully experienced the intended effect of the Preacher's words. His preference for silence is to be interpreted as a state of muteness induced by the absolute meaninglessness of history and the consequent emptiness of human life. Neither anger nor criticism can change a thing; so it is better just to be silent.

Situations may arise, however, in which it is better to speak than to be silent. If Christ has given a real meaning and destination to history, then we need not be paralyzed by nostalgia for that which is irrevocably past; we can give a meaningful shape to our lives here and now—and to the lives of our fellowmen. The light that radiates back to us from the future makes such expectancy and action possible. Therefore these things can also be talked about. It is precisely this change, which came after Ecclesiastes was written, that now needs to be proclaimed with a clear, loud voice—it is called the gospel. Out of this gospel something like a holy evangelical fury against lovelessness and injustice can arise. We need not accept what is wrong. The gospel will enable us to find our voices—not in foolish impulsiveness but with conviction as to what is good.

WISDOM AND POSSESSIONS 7:11-14

This poem consists of two parts that are clearly separable: verses 11 and 12 concern the advantage of wisdom, and verses

13 and 14 concern the work of God. Still, this is not a case in which two themes with little or nothing to do with each other have been patched together. That the two strophes occur together shows that they have some connection, and the Preacher does not disappoint us. It is by combining two unexpected themes that he transmits, with succinctness, his brief but powerful message.

He begins by making the unexpected remark that wisdom is a good thing when accompanied by possessions. Those who are still alive ("who see the sun") profit from this combination. This, we should think, is something everybody knows. But then he gives his reason for the statement: both wisdom and possessions have the character of a shelter. In life one can protect oneself with wisdom, and one can do the same with money as well. In this regard both are equally valuable and have the same effect. But then why does the Preacher start by saying that wisdom with possessions is a good thing? A person may, for example, have the protection of riches but lack wisdom. In that case he is at a disadvantage by comparison with one who has both. The latter enjoys an additional advantage that derives only from wisdom: wisdom preserves the life of its possessor. This is not to suggest that somehow wisdom confers on a person the capacity to escape or delay death (see 3:2, 19), still less that wisdom makes known to its possessor the way to a life hereafter; for such ideas are completely inconceivable to the Preacher, who expects no life after death. The advantage of wisdom over riches lies in that it confers gifts of life even when riches disappear. Riches do protect a person to a point, but when someone with only possessions loses them (see 5:14), his protection is gone too. But when someone with both wisdom and riches loses his possessions, then his protection is not totally wiped out. Herein lies the advantage of wisdom over money.

This praise of wisdom is especially striking here. The first strophe of the poem might just as well have been a part of Proverbs (compare verse 12b with Prov. 3:18, and this entire passage with Prov. 3:13-18). But here the Preacher links wisdom with other ideas so that these typical "words of wisdom" acquire a very different value. The beginning of the second strophe in verse 13 alludes to 1:15, where it says that what is crooked cannot possibly be straightened out. But now the Preacher adds a new element that must have totally nonplussed the early readers of the book: he says the crooked has been made so by God! He is the cause of it! And what is more, no man is able to make straight—that is, improve—what God has made crooked. God as the overruling supreme Power is pictured in even grimmer terms here: he not only *rules* over all, but according to the Preacher, everything is *his doing*. So we read, "Consider the work of God."

In any case, when you look closely at human wisdom, it is not very important, for there is nothing one can do about this "work of God." The only advice the Preacher can offer in the circumstances is that one must accept the situation as it is (v. 14). When times of prosperity arrive (as pictured in the favorable halves of 3:2-8), they must be accepted with joy; but when bad times come over you (as pictured in the unfavorable parts of 3:2-8), you must remember that God has caused these just as much as the prosperous times you have enjoyed. What all this comes down to is that even the wisest man cannot do a thing about it. The only conceivable posture one can adopt is a kind of mindless acceptance or mute resignation, for man can never tell what God has decided to do in the future. From this perspective, then, the knowledge of wisdom is not all that valuable.

Summary

We have here three sets of polar opposites:

Thought:	Wisdom
Counterthought:	Possessions
Tension:	Relative advantage of wisdom
Thought:	Wisdom
Counterthought:	The work of God
Tension:	Worthlessness of wisdom
Thought:	Times of prosperity
Counterthought:	Times of adversity
Tension:	Man lies helplessly in the hand of God

These ideas are no longer very strange to the reader who has read the book through from the beginning. But the Preacher has a way, even in cases where his theme is already familiar, of keeping the reader interested. The opposition of wisdom and riches or prosperity and adversity is already un-

settling, but the choice of words by which the Preacher underscores a previously mentioned idea, namely, that God is the
cause of it all, really upsets the reader. If God preordains all
things, he also preordains evil! For that reason there can be
no real human responsibility: all things lie in the hand of
God. This is the source of the Preacher's tired acceptance of
all that happens and his reserved attitude toward life in general. A God-concept like his has profound consequences for
one's worldview and life-style.

What must we make of it? It is plain that the foundations
of the Christian faith are threatened here. For us to adopt this
God-concept would mean that we could no longer believe
Christianly. Sin would no longer entail guilt; man would no
longer be responsible to God; the work of Christ would be
superfluous. We cannot avoid this train of consequences by
escaping aboard the pious idea that adversity can be a means
by which God disciplines us. For the Preacher holds his reader
captive in the tense domain of futility: man is simply prey to
the arbitrariness of God.

The solution, again, lies in Christ. By his coming he has
demonstrated that there is more to be known of God than
there was in the time of the Preacher; that God is not just a
capricious apportioner of human fortune; that everything that
happens, though subject to his rule, is by no means always
his will; and that people have to render an account of their
doings.

We can now still be happy in days of prosperity, but in
times of adversity we need no longer, in resignation, lie down
before the superior Power. We can draw near to him and pray
to him for help. Although he is in heaven and we are on earth
(5:2), there is now a way open to him (John 14:6). Therefore
there is now a wisdom and there are now riches whose value
is absolute and not relative (see 1 Cor. 1:30; Eph. 1:17-18).

NO HAPPY MEDIUM 7:15-22

The Preacher begins by saying that he has seen "everything."
That is not to be taken as a literal reference to everything there
is to be observed on earth, but it refers to the two possibilities
mentioned in verse 15. Often a righteous man perishes de-

spite his righteousness, and often a wicked man, despite his wickedness, enjoys the blessing of a long life, a blessing that to those in the East was particularly desirable. Not order but chaos prevails in human life. That is a subject that greatly torments the Preacher. This state of affairs means that the doctrine of retribution becomes nonoperational—another way of saying that the most fundamental basis of wisdom literature cannot be accepted either. For established wisdom operates on the premise—and the promise—that correct and orderly conduct is rewarded and that incorrect conduct is punished. But here the reverse is true. The consequences of this for the precepts of the wisdom teachers are now made explicit in the famous (or, depending on the reader's orientation, infamous) verses 16 and 17.

Here we encounter an antilogion, an expression in which it seems that two opposites directly contradict each other. Closer scrutiny will show, however, that there is no inner contradiction here. In verse 16 the Preacher offers the prescription not to be righteous overmuch and also not to be overly wise. In accordance with the best-established convention of Hebrew poetry, namely, the parallelism of parts, righteousness and wisdom should mean the same thing—something that is corroborated by the book of Proverbs. Verse 17 conveys the prescription not to be wicked overmuch and not to be a fool. Again we have two parallel pronouncements that show that the wicked man and the fool are the same to the Preacher—this is also verifiable by the standards of generally accepted usage. This should caution us against the oversimple assumption that the Preacher is here advocating some sin or other. In both instances he warns against the excessive pursuit of righteousness/wisdom and wickedness/folly. A superficial reading of this passage might lead one to think that his interest lies in advocating the wisdom of everyman: the wisdom of the golden mean. And in fact these verses are often misunderstood that way.

The solution to the problem is to be found in the rhetorical questions at the end of each verse. By means of these questions the Preacher advances the thesis that destruction and ruin follow extreme righteousness/wisdom as well as their opposites. Even the highest reaches of wisdom cannot control human fortune, and of course neither can the excesses of folly. So we have here, in minuscule form, a view like the one we encountered earlier in the grand experiment with wisdom and folly (1:12–2:26). Neither wisdom nor folly deserves commendation. Besides, there are also indications that these pronouncements cannot be meant as a defense of the golden mean. One cannot argue that if overmuch righteousness is wrong then moderate righteousness is good, or that if overmuch wickedness is wrong then moderate wickedness is good. The Preacher is a radical thinker; his convictions are always all-embracing and thorough—to him *all* is vanity. It would be strange, then, if he should deviate here from his fundamental conviction.

Next follows verse 18, in which the Preacher says it is good if man grasps the one as well as the other (NIV, cf. RSV). This can refer only to the two admonitions of the previous two verses. For if man cannot insure well-being and prosperity for himself by being righteous (= being a wise man), he cannot avail himself of salvation in the opposite direction either. He who fears God, he who really takes account of the reality of God, escapes both dangers (cf. RSV: "he . . . shall come forth from them all."). What is the author referring to? Certainly not to some moderate sin. It would be contradictory if the Preacher first summoned people into the direction of moderate sin, as some interpreters think he does in verses 16 and 17, and then pictured the escape from it as something good. Nor can he mean that the person who fears God will escape misfortune, for that is a singular concept and the author says expressly that he who fears God will escape both (a plural concept). In other words, he is referring only to the two admonitions of verses 16 and 17. Verse 18a refers to these too: one should hold to the warning against excessive righteousness and to that against excessive wickedness. Then you will avoid both dangers: that of seeking your own salvation in wisdom (by obeying all its precepts, v. 16) as well as that of trying to find your well-being in folly (by committing the opposite of righteousness, v. 17).

Verse 19 is a parenthesis (almost casually inserted) between verses 15-18 and verses 20-22. This means that verse 18 links up directly with verse 20 which tells us why nothing good is to be gained from extreme wisdom or folly. The reason is simply that no one on earth has that capacity. This idea occurs also in other passages in the Old Testament (e.g., 1 Kings 8:46; Pss. 14 and 130; and, in wisdom literature itself,

Job 15:14-16 and Prov. 20:9). The Preacher is not explaining a doctrine of original sin but simply asserting as his starting point that no man is always able to act correctly. "Sinful" for him means only that a person is sometimes incorrect in the things he does or fails to do.

The final four lines (vv. 21-22) illustrate this all-embracing thesis with an example. As he loves to do (cf. vv. 16-17), the Preacher puts his words in the form of an admonition, entirely in the style of the wisdom teachers with whom he has such profound differences. He also at this point addresses the reader directly: You. His advice is that you must not pay attention to what people say among each other about you, for then you might hear a lowly slave cursing you—and that is not a pleasant experience. But the real point lies not in the unpleasant shock to one's system resulting from the curse but in the warning that the one cursed must not be angry over the insult because if he is honest he must admit that he has done precisely the same thing to others. This direct address here means there is general validity in what he says: everyone who hears another cursing him is himself guilty of the same thing—many times over! In other words, there is no one who only acts correctly.

Meanwhile, we have bypassed the parenthesis of verse 19. In this verse wisdom is applauded and even commended! Wisdom is so powerful that a wise man is stronger than ten mighty rulers in a fortified city. This statement is precisely the opposite of the dark picture the Preacher just painted a moment before, but it is not, as commentators often suppose, a later interpolation that breaks up the sequence. Such a parenthesis, which seems only to disturb the sequence of thought between the preceding and the following words, can also be found in verses 10:4 and 8:12b-13. The Preacher can be extremely careful in his choice of words and with the structure of his poems, as we have often seen (e.g., 3:2-8). Unfortunately his wordplays cannot be reproduced in English. The word translated "for" (KJV) with which verse 20 begins can also mean "but" in Hebrew. So there are two possible readings of the text—one without the parenthesis and the other with the parenthesis of verse 19. If we read directly from verse 18 to verse 20 we can paraphrase as follows: "He who takes account of God escapes both possibilities of misconstruing his own capacities, *for* there is no man on earth whose capacity enables him to act correctly." If we now include the parenthesis in our reading of the text, we can reproduce the sequence as follows: "Wisdom gives power to a man, *but* all men on earth are devoid of inner strength." The effect of this ingenious wordplay is that the Preacher brings out what, according to him, true wisdom is. Truly wise is only the one who knows what little value wisdom has.

So this poem agrees completely with the general tenor of the book. Perhaps the opposition to accepted wisdom is accentuated a little on account of the two meanings that verse 19 can have. By itself this verse expresses the fond praises with which wisdom loves to commend itself. In this case, the idea of the surpassing power of wisdom, an idea that is dear to the wisdom teachers (cf. Prov. 6:32; 21:22; 24:5-6), has been taken over. But in this context it serves as an unmasking statement exposing the weakness of wisdom. The Preacher shows that only his wisdom can claim to be strong, for he knows that all human capacity is weak.

Summary

Thought:	Wisdom
Counterthought:	Chaos in life
Tension:	Worthlessness of wisdom

And

Thought:	The Preacher's wise opinion
Counterthought:	Generally accepted wisdom
Tension:	Relative advantage of the Preacher's wisdom

The last person in the Bible who would recommend the golden mean is the Preacher. One cannot therefore appeal to this poem in defense of it (better for that purpose is Prov. 25:16, 27). Nor can we say that the Preacher is prepared to accept moderate sin. This, in all likelihood, will not trouble the reader of the Bible. But what forces us to halt is the bitterly ironic point of view that the only true wisdom consists in the denial that any wisdom exists among men. The irrevocable finality and the stark pessimism of this viewpoint are not things we can share. But in our Christian context we can let this theme of the Preacher function in a new way (the same technique he himself likes to apply to others!). We can and do say that those who have not come to realize the utter inadequacy of their own abilities, knowledge, and wisdom can never attain to true wisdom—the wisdom to use all their abilities in the service of God. The true order is first the consciousness of total bankruptcy and then the riches of meaningful service. For in between these two occurs the intervention of Christ, who gives strength—more than all the rulers in a thousand cities.

BITTER WISDOM 7:23–8:1

Both the boundaries of this passage and its inner development are disputed. But 8:1 has to be the conclusion of the passage that precedes it because from 8:2 on a totally new theme begins (political powerlessness), to which there is no reference in 7:23–8:1. Furthermore, since there is mention of the same subject (wisdom) in 7:23 and in 8:1, these two verses enclose a unified whole.

When we look more closely at the structure of this passage it turns out to be something like that of the grand experiment of 1:12–2:26. This, too, is the story of an experiment with wisdom and folly. Verses 23-25 form the introduction that announces the test; verses 26-28 report the result (introduced by the words "I find"); and the four lines of the last two verses offer the summary ("I found").

Verse 23 states the purpose of the experiment. The Preacher has striven to be really wise, but that wisdom was unattainable to him. Naturally he is not talking about the accepted wisdom of the teachers—he was thoroughly familiar with that—nor simply about his own insights, in the light of which he criticizes his colleagues in wisdom circles. Rather, he is talking about the true wisdom that can offer truly satisfying solutions to the riddles of life (among many such, the reversal of the law of retribution, with which he dealt in the preceding poem). That which is—that is, life's bewildering reality—is far off and extremely deep (v. 24); the verse ends with a rhetorical question whose meaning is that no one can discover the explanation of reality. At the very beginning, then, the Preacher refers to the negative outcome of his experiment, as he did in the case of his earlier grand experiment (cf. 1:13ff.).

But this time also the reverse of wisdom is subjected to scrutiny (v. 25). Here too we note that "wicked" and "foolish" are synonymous (cf. 7:17) and do not describe moral and intellectual aberration or failure. Unlike a similar undertaking in the case of the grand experiment, the investigation of folly is not described at length (cf. 2:1-11).

The result of the enterprise immediately follows in verse 26. But the Preacher does not report it in a prosaic way: he uses an example that illustrates, rather than announces, the outcome. It is the well-known example of the loose woman of whom we hear so often in wisdom literature generally (e.g., Prov. 2:16-19; 5:1ff.; 7:6ff.; 23:27-28; and numerous other texts from Israel, Egypt, and Mesopotamia). Again and again the teachers warn against the dangers that threaten the young man who associates with such women. They offer the prescriptions of wisdom on how to avoid the loose woman and the misfortune she brings with her. But the Preacher has another point of view. He who is well pleasing to God will escape the loose woman, and he who is not well pleasing to God will be caught in her snare. This favor of God simply comes over a person or fails to come—those are the chances of life over which one has no control (see 3:1-9; 5:18-20; 6:1-2). In other words, it is not wisdom but God who determines who will go free and who will not. The example of the loose woman illustrates, therefore, that in general the prescriptions of wisdom have no value. This is one of the clearest cases where the Preacher takes a typical idea of accepted wisdom and uses it against the intent of the general teaching. Verse 27 is proof that this polemic is important to him. Step by step, adding one thing to another, he has worked toward a conclusion. We hardly needed this assurance, though. One who has seen how precise his observations are, how sharp his eye and how thorough his argumentation, knows that this is a thinker worthy of the name.

The Preacher could have left it at that but he adds two more lines on the subject of women (v. 28). This is difficult poetry, but razor sharp. He says that he has searched for a long time. That is, he has long searched for a good woman in the true sense of the word but has not found even one among a thousand. This means there is none. Among a thousand people perhaps one good person can be found, but it is not a woman. One cannot draw a conclusion from this exception (for instance, that the Preacher still assumes that the perfect person exists) since this talk is only a sharp way of saying that no such (good) woman exists. It is approximately this kind of reasoning that Paul uses in Romans 5:7-8. But this extremely negative pronouncement on women by no means signifies that the Preacher is a woman hater. On the contrary, in 9:9 he expresses his appreciation for women. What we have here is an exaggeration with a literary purpose (cf. 4:1, 4, 15, where the same technique is used). In the previous verses the special case of the loose woman showed just that the prescriptions of wisdom are useless. By according all women such negative status the Preacher emphasizes that the case of the "woman" poses an unavoidable danger to the wise man. This is how he mocks the accepted wisdom, in which the appreciation for the good woman is just as prevalent as the criticism of a loose woman (e.g., Prov. 18:22; 19:14; 31:10ff.).

The author summarizes his reflections in the last four lines (7:29–8:1). God has made human beings upright, of one piece, uncomplicated. But rather than accepting their simplicity they have invented clever schemes. The word for "clever schemes" ("devices," RSV) in the Hebrew bears a similarity to the word for "the result of wisdom"—by which we can tell that the Preacher in fact thinks little of accepted wisdom. People have conceived all sorts of clever schemes in order to try to evade the inevitable—that, according to the Preacher, is what all the prescriptions of wisdom come down to. It would have been better if people had remained uncomplicated and simple.

But all of a sudden this train of thought turns in an opposite direction. The last verse of the poem (8:1) contains several positive pronouncements on wisdom. "Who is like the wise man?" is the rhetorical question, and the implied answer is that no one can be compared to him. The following rhetorical question is really a thesis that only the wise man knows the explanation of the problems of life. In addition, wisdom has a wholesome effect on the wise man that can even be seen on his face. This combination of opposites is not strange to the reader of these poems. In the present context, however, this verse is a veiled reference to the Preacher himself and to his own wisdom. We have just been told that wisdom is worth so little that it would have been better if people had been left in a state of nondevelopment. Who then is the true wise man, and who has the true answers to the problem? He who knows that wisdom is worthless and who therefore accepts the position that God, in his distribution of human fortunes (v. 26b), cannot be fathomed.

Summary

Thought:	Wisdom
Counterthought:	God's sovereign apportionment
Tension:	Worthlessness of wisdom

But all this distills the wise opinions of the Preacher, so

Thought:	The wisdom of the Preacher
Counterthought:	Generally accepted wisdom
Tension:	The relative advantage of the Preacher's wisdom

The Preacher regards the loose woman as undesirable, as is evident from the negative role she plays in his example. But his concern is hardly to offer a moral evaluation of sexual behavior, for the loose woman is simply an illustration of the uselessness of the rule that wisdom laid down. Nor can one, in the interest of discriminating against women, appeal to the Preacher's assertion that there is no good woman, for that too is a literary technique with which he attacks wisdom in general. One would come closer to the correct interpretation of the poem by saying that it is wise to realize how little man knows. But that must be qualified by the warning that the Preacher does not mean to promote some sort of wholesome intellectual modesty. For him everything depends on the arbitrary apportionments of God, not on human wisdom.

For the Christian believer everything depends on the *gracious* and *loving* apportionments of God, as a result of which human wisdom and moral responsibility again get their full worth.

POLITICAL POWER AND POWERLESSNESS 8:2-9

The Preacher sketches the main thrust of the passage in the first strophe (vv. 2-4); next he unfolds his line of reasoning (vv. 5-8); and finally he offers a summary (v. 9).

He begins with an admonition to obey the king "because of your sacred oath." This last clause can be interpreted in numerous ways. The oath may be one made before God in fidelity to the king, or an oath made before the king, who was then considered a god (something that happened in pagan antiquity), or even the oath demanded in a court of law. It could also mean an oath that God swears before a king, though this is extremely unlikely because here the Preacher discusses only heathen kings. Finally, it can be an oath that God requires of the king's subjects. Because this last possibility fits best with the expansion in the second strophe, we deem it the most likely. So the king must be obeyed because God requires it. The king has political power at his disposal and his subjects are politically powerless because God has let it turn out that way.

Tied in with this situation is an ambivalent admonition. Verse 3 can mean one of two things. It may mean that it is better to refrain from hastily going before the king, in a law-suit for instance, and to leave the king's presence, than it is to stand up for a bad cause in the dangerous atmosphere of the royal court (see RSV). For the king is a despot; misfortune may await the person who, in the king's opinion, has adopted the wrong viewpoint. It is also possible, however, to translate the Hebrew as follows: "Do not be in a hurry to leave the king's presence" (NIV), which would mean that the Preacher here warns against any rebellion by which one would break one's relationship with the king. This second view appears to be the less preferable translation (the idea of haste would be superfluous—would the Preacher be opposed only to hasty rebellion?). In any case, no matter how one translates it, the implication of verse 3 remains the same in light of the context: the king can do what he pleases (v. 3c) and no one can call him to account (v. 4). In this manner the Preacher stresses the political supremacy of the king and the total powerlessness of the subject. In the first strophe, then, the author recommends a posture that is politically introspective. Again he has taken on a well-known theme in wisdom literature: the power of the king (cf. Prov. 14:35; 16:13-15; 25:3), but already here it becomes plain that the author is displaying his customary pessimism.

Verse 5, which opens the second part, sounds so much like the official wisdom that some commentators view it as a later insertion by a copyist. But it is not so simple. Again the Preacher is citing current wisdom with the idea of attacking it. By itself verse 5 sounds like a proverb on how a wise man acts at the royal court: obediently, so that no harm comes to him, with a good sense of timing. The same applies to verse 6: there is a proper time for everything, and although life is safe for no man, he can make it a lot more secure by choosing his way with intelligence. This is what the wise men taught their disciples.

But when the readers reach verse 7 they realize that there is a shift in subject matter. The teachers of wisdom assume all kinds of possibilities in man but the Preacher emphasizes only the ignorance of everything that is alive. For that reason the preceding verses cannot mean that people who make the right decisions at the right time can maintain themselves in the king's presence; they mean rather that the true wise man knows he has to show restraint before the king's authority since time (which is in God's hands) may hold a bad fate for him. So why obey the king? Not because he is a servant of God (Rom. 13:4) but because no one can really resist the irrevocably fixed circumstances of life (3:1-9)—not even in politics.

In verse 8, to make sure that we shall understand him correctly the Preacher adds four examples of the powerlessness of man: no one can contain the wind; no one can determine the day of his death; no one can get exemption from military service (cf. Deut. 20:5ff.) under a king who does precisely what he pleases; and even riches carry no weight against a political power. In this last instance (riches) a tiny scribal error has crept in. The letters of the word for "riches" and those of the word for "wickedness" are almost identical, which is why several translations (KJV, RSV, NIV) speak of wickedness rather than of riches. This series of examples cuts off every possibility that the reader might still think that ordinary subjects have some power at their disposal. Of course a king cannot contain the wind either, or determine the day of his death, but this implication does not play a role in the poetic design of the author. His concern is only to stress the idea of powerlessness, so that it can put a damper on every optimistic misconception and serve as counterpole to royal supremacy.

Finally the Preacher sums up his reflections (v. 9). According to him people are in opposition to each other politically: the one exercises power at the expense of the other. He is therefore critical of the political structures of his day. Monarchial authority should serve the interests of the people (see 10:17), but in reality it functions to their hurt. But he does not utter his protest against such exercise of power. Although he regards God as the ultimate cause of the situation, there is no hint here of the notion that the king is obligated to carry out the will of God (cf. Deut. 17:14-20). The gap between the Preacher and the prophets is as large as the gap between him and the established teachers of wisdom (cf. 1 Sam. 12:1ff.; 1 Kings 13:1ff.; 16:1ff.; 18:18ff.; Isa. 7:10-17; etc.). Instead of announcing God's judgment upon such a hurtful exercise of power, he resigns himself to the idea that God has determined the nature of despotism (v. 2) and he describes only what he has observed in life around him (v. 9).

Summary

Thought:	Political power
Counterthought:	Political powerlessness
Tension:	Abandonment to an unfavorable situation

But such political arrangements are the result of divine dispensations. Therefore,

Thought:	God's apportionment
Counterthought:	Conduct of subjects
Tension:	Resigned acceptance, without protest

In many respects the Preacher's poems are quite "modern," in that his critical and analytical view of life and society occurs very frequently today as well. His topics, too, sound contemporary: knowledge, wealth, social injustice, corruption, and the distribution of political power. In another and important respect, however, he is totally at odds with the modern view—that is, in his passivity and resigned acceptance of the status quo. This combination surfaces nowhere more clearly than in his poem on political power. Even the double impression the Preacher makes on the present-day reader resembles a bipolar pattern filled with tension!

The theology of liberation, at least in its political dimensions, cannot expect to get any help from the Preacher in designing a program of action. He would only say of it: "vanity and a chasing after wind." But that does not make this anti-activistic book irrelevant, leaving us only the flaming words of the prophets to motivate us to relate our faith to the political arena. In at least one way the Preacher's radical analysis of political reality is of importance: he reveals that the people in power (not only kings—verse 9b is more general) use their power to the hurt of others. When a person makes this discovery in the world, he can justify his lethargy and inactivity in one of two ways. Either he can view it from a pre-Christian perspective, which would mean that he took no account of the coming of Christ into the world; or he can close his eyes to the actual situation by picturing it as being prettier than it really is, which would mean that he probably wanted to enjoy the advantages of the existing political situation and so had to justify his own political position from a Christian perspective.

But the true Christian response to the Preacher takes a different turn. In the first instance Christ will have to be proclaimed, so that it may be evident that in him the whole world has become a meaningful domain in which to live and work. In the second instance the implications of Christ's claim upon the totality of life will have to be preached, so that it may be evident that the political realities may not be excluded from the dynamic field of his demands. This also implies a call to manysidedness and balance. Political preaching cannot be the whole of the preacher's task. It is not the only thing that matters. This too the Preacher knows—does he not speak, in his own way, about life and death and love?

DOES JUSTICE EXIST IN THE WORLD? 8:10-15

The first strophe (v. 10) poses the fundamental problem of wisdom literature; the second (vv. 11-12a) states a consequence of it. In verses 12b-13 the same parenthesis occurs as in 7:19 and 10:4, and the entire problem is repeated in the fourth strophe (v. 14). The conclusion is one of five instances in which the Preacher offers his famous recommendation to enjoy life.

At the start we encounter the same sort of scribal error we observed in 8:8, by which the letters of a word have been changed around by a copyist. The reference is to a wicked person who *draws near* (see NEB), not to one who has been *buried* (as KJV, RSV, NIV, and TEV have it).* "Drawing near" is a technical term for participation in worship in the sanctuary, and in fact the same verse mentions "the holy place." If we were to take the text to refer to a funeral, this parallel statement would imply that the cemetery is holy; and that is not the case. Actually, the Preacher is describing a fundamental observation of the idea of retribution. Just as in 7:26 he used an illustration, so here too he elucidates the principle with an example, this time one that is taken from the sphere of worship. Wicked people are allowed to draw near and take part in the cultic process; but good people, whose conduct has been just, have to leave the sanctuary. Besides, they are forgotten by the entire city—a particularly unfortunate fate for one from the ancient East (cf. 1:11; 9:15-16). So where one would expect expulsion from the sanctuary, admission occurs; and where admission might be expected, there is not only expulsion, but ostracism, rejection, and banishment from the community. This shows that the theory of retribution does not work, and by demonstrating this, the illustration knocks the bottom out of wisdom literature. For that reason, the Preacher concludes the strophe with his well-known declaration of futility.

The doctrine of retribution teaches that a good deed is rewarded and a bad deed punished. This is the prevailing concept in the Old Testament—in the law as well as in the evaluation of history espoused in the book of Kings, from the Psalms to the judgment upon Israel proclaimed by the prophets. In wisdom literature the doctrine of retribution ties in with the idea of a divine order. By integrating himself into this order (i.e., by keeping the rules of wisdom), a person enters into harmony with the will of God and God rewards him. But if a person ignores the rules that govern this process of integration, he clashes with the divine order and God punishes him. Examples of this teaching may be seen throughout the book of Proverbs, especially from chapter 10 on.

*The author's translation of verse 10, which shows further differences from the major English translations, reads as follows: "Likewise I saw wicked men draw near and enter, while they ought to go out of the holy place; and in the city are forgotten those who have acted justly. This too is vanity."— Trans.

If the Preacher now comes and proves in a case study, as it were, that this crucial supporting pillar of wisdom cannot be trusted, he shakes the foundation of the entire religion of ancient Israel as a theology of merit—and that foundation, according to the Preacher, is nothing but an illusion! In order to reinforce his opinion, he continues to reason on that basis (v. 11). Why is man forever inclined to do evil? Because the sentence, which retribution theory says should then come, is not carried out speedily. Apparently humanity does not fear its own idea of retribution—that, in effect, is what verse 11 says—and what kind of religious conviction is that?

In case someone still questions the results of his research, wondering about their general validity, there is still the more comprehensive and general phenomenon that a wicked man can commit any number of evil deeds and nevertheless experience the blessing of a long life (v. 12a). No explanation can be offered for this; it cannot be viewed as a rare exception, for it happens a hundred times (i.e., continually); nor can the problem be solved, as some think (see Pss. 37:10; 49:16ff.; 73:18ff.), by hoping for a sudden turnaround at the end, because the point of the example is precisely that the wicked man may be blessed throughout his life. Moreover, the formulations of the Preacher are again so precise and razor sharp that the escape from a future judgment as described in 3:17 is cut off. He said that sentencing of an evil deed does not take place *speedily*. That is, at some time or other, it will come. But the testimony of the opening strophe and of the later examples is so uniform that they cannot mean anything good— as though the Preacher still expected a righteous judgment sooner or later that would sometime, somewhere give meaning to life. This notion would also clash with the superscription (1:2) and the postscript (12:8) to the entire book. As in 3:17 the final judgment is death, which—though it may not be immediate—does come. And that is a bitter irony, for to the author death is not an entrance into a better life, but merely the same end—nonexistence—of both the good and the evil (see 3:20; 9:3). The death sentence comes upon all. In this way the Preacher only emphasizes anew that a just punishment-and-reward theory does not work.

The absence of just retribution is supported by further proofs in verse 14, but before we get to them, in the middle of the poem—surrounded before and after by two strophes—

we are offered an excellent formulation of the very theory the Preacher is busy attacking (vv. 12b-13). According to this theory it will go well with those who reverence God, that is, those who consider themselves bound by the general precepts of wisdom, *because* they keep the precepts; and it will go ill with the "wicked," those who disregard wisdom, *because* they commit such wrong deeds. That is the clearest and simplest way to propagate the doctrine of retribution.

Especially the latter element has a clear function: the wicked man, according to this view, will not enjoy a long life. But the Preacher has said expressly in verse 12a that in fact he has seen the opposite happen. Because of the tension between this passage and the rest of the poem there are again some exegetes who regard the passage as a later insertion by a conservative editor and therefore label it nonauthentic. But one cannot treat the passage as an insertion by a glossator, for when the author says in verse 12b, "yet I know," he uses a different form of the Hebrew verb from that used when he offers his own opinion. What he is doing is this: he cites the anticipated answer to the first part of his argument in advance in order to torpedo it in the last part. Something similar occurs also in certain Greek philosophers and in the letters of Paul and James when they anticipate objections to their opinions and answer them in advance (see Rom. 9:19; 11:19; 1 Cor. 15:35; James 2:18). And really not much is left of these pious-sounding words when the Preacher sets them up in opposition to his solid supply of life observations. For that reason the RSV (and also KJV and NIV) must surely be in error at this point when it makes the Preacher contradict himself in verses 12 and 13 (the wicked will prolong his days; the wicked will not prolong his days).

Verse 14 is very ingenious in its composition, as the Preacher uses both form and content to heighten the impact of his attack on the doctrine of retribution. He begins the strophe (a quatrain) with a declaration of futility: that which is about to be described is vain. He also ends the quatrain with a declaration of futility: that which was just written is vain. This double declaration conveys an extremely strong conviction. Between these two single lines of verse stand the two three-part lines that say that the doctrine of retribution proceeds crosswise: the righteous get what the wicked deserve and the wicked get what the righteous deserve. This X-pattern of retribution and reward is most artfully expressed in a verbal construction in which the words are also arranged in an X-pattern (chiasma):

first part—righteous   third part—wicked
first part—wicked   third part—righteous

The reader will recall the use of similar patterns in 3:2-8. Thus, with great consistency and poetic skill, the Preacher works out his case against the fundamental conviction of general wisdom, so that all counterarguments are invalidated.

After such a fundamental knockout of fashionable thought, there remains space only for the conclusion that needs to be drawn from all this. The Preacher still has to answer the question, "Now what?" The answer comes in the last strophe (verse 15). The only way out is to make the most of pleasure and feasting amid all the toil—as long as one can by the grace of God. The link between the happy tone of the conclusion and the preceding is the *negative* idea that God is the giver. That, one must realize, is not a positive idea, for God remains for the Preacher the inscrutable apportioner of an unpredictable fate, in which continuity and quiet confidence are equally unthinkable.

Summary

Thought:	Right conduct
Counterthought:	Wrong conduct
Tension:	No retribution, only meaninglessness

A Reformed Christian will perhaps read with pleasure how the Preacher demolishes, step by step, the doctrine of merit (the theory of retribution) and how he then demonstrates that not one stone remains on another. To that extent one can believe that no one who has read Ecclesiastes can continue to insist on an unproblematic doctrine of merit.

But, as usual, that is not where the Preacher's views end or cease to be relevant. If we agree that man, because of his sin, has no merit before God and can only appeal to him for grace, we have still not touched the question of God's justice. That is the problem with which the entire book of Job struggles. Is God just when the fates of human beings are applied crosswise—the fate of one imposed on another? Can one possibly acknowledge the existence of God's justice when one can observe so many counterinstances in life that make the position of the Preacher plausible? The answer, for him, is simply no.

For that reason his enjoy-yourself-if-you-can conclusion is all that remains. He no longer struggles with his God-concept by asking, for instance, why God allows so much injustice and even apportions it; for him God is too high and too despotic to be questioned by human beings on those points. The book of Job confronts the same problem and fails to find a satisfactory solution; yet Job's answer to the question whether God's justice is real is nevertheless yes. The reason is that his God-concept differs from that of the Preacher. For him, too, God is very high and powerful, but that is precisely why he can ultimately accept these apparent contradictions in life— just as we accept others for which God is responsible in creation (see Job 38:1ff.; 42:1ff.)—without blaming him. So that is a leap of faith in the direction of God. But the Preacher cannot make this jump over the yawning gap between earth and heaven (5:2), and consequently his thoughts remain stuck in the tensions of meaninglessness.

We can say, then, that in Ecclesiastes the question concerning the existence or nonexistence of God's justice illustrates the misery of humanity as a dead-end street, while in Job the question demonstrates what kind of leap of faith is needed to be rescued from the tensions of life. Often justice does not exist on earth—thanks to man. But the fact that God permits injustice need not lead us to believe that he is the source and apportioner of unjust life arrangements. That conclusion was already avoidable in the time of the Old Testament, as Job shows; yet it was still understandable, as Ecclesiastes shows. God allows things to happen that are contrary to his will; thus he is not responsible for them. But he maintains meaningful control over them in a way we cannot fathom, any more than we can fathom the creation, and he does this for his own purpose.

With these honest and radically consistent ideas the Preacher is particularly valuable on still another level. He, the radical spirit, who ascribes arbitrariness and even injustice to God, fulfills the role of a "schoolmaster to Christ." With this radical thinker in the Bible we can freely invite radical thinkers to join the church. They need not leave the holy place and be forgotten in the city (cf. 8:10).

THE INSCRUTABILITY OF GOD'S WORK 8:16-17

This poem constitutes the link between the preceding (8:10-15) and the following (9:1-10) poems, where in both instances the subject is the doctrine of retribution. In these two adjoining passages human action in general is contrasted with divine action; and in the present intervening piece human wisdom in particular is contrasted with God's work.

Again, the Preacher refers to an assignment he has given himself. He has sought to get to know the wisdom of mankind and its toilsome labor. There is something peculiar and compulsive about human wisdom and labor; people can busy themselves with them without allowing themselves any rest. Had the author spoken only of sleeplessness at night, his mention of this characteristic would not have struck us, for as a rule when one discusses sleeplessness one usually means that at night. Under certain circumstances, of course, this is natural. But now that he speaks also of sleeplessness during the day he is implying that there is deep-rooted unrest in man—there is no rest in the never-ending labor that man, with the wisdom given him, tries to accomplish. Here the idea of human labor (cf. 3:10-15; 4:4-6; 4:7-12) overshadows that of wisdom. Now what is so extraordinary about this tension-filled phenomenon? That is the question the Preacher has put to himself.

Now comes the answer. When he examined this phenomenon, he saw all that God had done. Beneath the labor done in the domain of human wisdom is the activity of God. Therefore it is important to place a colon after the first line of verse 17 ("Then I saw all the work of God: . . ."). The colon stands for a Hebrew word that indicates that the "incomprehensibles" of life referred to in the following three lines are the work of God. He means to say, not that he has observed all the work that God has ever done, but that the riddle he has seen must be attributed to God's action.

The following lines state bluntly that the work of God is inaccessible to the human mind. The term *find out* is used with regularity in all three lines. But there is also a noticeable progression. The first line says only that man cannot comprehend what goes on in life. The second line reinforces the idea, for here the Preacher says that man's inability to understand cannot be overcome by searching things out, however intense the effort. The last line takes the argument one step further: although the wise man claims he can explain the processes of life, that is not so—even he cannot see a pattern in them. At this point the Preacher openly challenges accepted wisdom in general. That kind of wisdom always claimed "to know" and "to understand" (cf. Prov. 1:2). The wisdom teachers had the belief that with their system they could judge all things and that they could uncover a patterned regularity in God's dealings with life. It is on this premise that the doctrine of retribution—the basis of the surrounding poems—is built. To be considered wise in the art of living a man must always follow this pattern. The Preacher, for his part, not only suggests that this theory is unacceptable but says in so many words that the wisdom teachers have not discovered any part of God's work and that the entire substructure of their movement therefore rests on a false claim.

But the Preacher is not a haughty critic. The final conclusion of the entire poem shows that his wisdom also falls in the category of the worthless. He undertook a "wisdom" initiative in order to arrive at comprehension. But all he has found out is that he cannot find out a thing about God's work—that it is incomprehensible. So his wisdom fares no better than that of the teachers in general. His only advantage over them lies in that he at least knows how unfathomable God's action in life is, whereas they wrongly think they know the action itself. So the element of relativity plays an important role here. Depending on the concept with which the wisdom of the Preacher is compared or related, it is either valuable or worthless.

Summary

Thought: General wisdom
Counterthought: God's work
Tension: General wisdom is unable to explain and is therefore worthless

Now that is the wise opinion of the Preacher; therefore,

Thought: General wisdom
Counterthought: The Preacher's wisdom
Tension: Relative advantage of the Preacher's
                       wisdom

But when the Preacher's wisdom faces the work of God it fares no better than wisdom in general:

Thought: The Preacher's wisdom
Counterthought: God's work
Tension: Worthlessness of the Preacher's
                       wisdom

The unrest and tensions that imbue the Preacher's thoughts grow so strong in this poem that they take possession of the serious reader. To some degree the criticism in them—the sobering attack on the self-sufficiency of human conceptual schemes that tend to confer the illusion of knowledge—is wholesome. However piously intended, every system that claims to be binding even for God is untrue. Today no wisdom teacher—or, to use the modern term, no theologian—will admit that he thinks God is bound to follow patterned regularity of any kind. The question, however, is whether in his actual world of belief he does in fact regard God as a God bound by a system. Not only the collection of ideas we find in the works of ancient Eastern teachers of wisdom but also those ideas we call a confession can function like a computer program of faith that spits out all the answers on request. To understand the Preacher is at least to be cured of the tendency to systematize God, and it is to learn to accept less than speedy solutions to real problems.

But there is a reverse side to his wholesome criticism. For all our appreciation of the Preacher we have to admit he leaves us in a state of unrest. He smashes our programmed computer-faith but also submits his own alternative as being worthless. Where imaginary wisdom once ruled, a vacuum remains that bears the name "vanity" in Ecclesiastes. That is the reverse side of his beneficial criticism.

But even this unrest and tension the author creates in us may be of value. For it is a negative indication that man's knowledge of God must come from another source. Though man by wisdom did not come to know God (1 Cor. 1:21), he may come to know God because God revealed himself (Matt. 16:17). This self-disclosure of God is not a philosophical system or a list of rules but a human being. For that reason, to know God is not a matter of exploration and explanation but a matter of trust and fellowship. Anyone who believes in Christ knows him and anyone who knows him knows the Father (John 14:7).

THERE IS NO RETRIBUTION 9:1-10

This poem consists of three clearly defined parts. Verses 1 and 2 concern the Preacher's observations of the equality of the fate of all men; verses 3-6 contain the conclusions he has drawn from them; and verses 7-10 form the well-known enjoy-yourself-if-you-can conclusion to which he has come on the basis of the preceding.

Although the Hebrew text of verse 1 is not altogether certain, the general thrust is fortunately clear enough that we can establish the author's original intent with reasonable certainty.

This verse is a very clear expression of the idea that all human enterprises are subordinate to God. Even the righteous and the wise are in God's hand. This does not mean they are safe and secure; it means they are in God's power. A person knows nothing of the most fundamental qualities of his own deeds and cannot say whether a given deed is an expression of love or hate. The implication is that he cannot have any influence on his own work. The only alternative is that everything has been predetermined by God; that is the import of the sentence beginning at the end of verse 1 and ending at the beginning of verse 2 [the author translates: "All is predestined; all is (vanity); for one fate befalls all"; cf. RSV]. This idea occurs repeatedly in Ecclesiastes (cf. 1:9, 15; 3:1-9, 14-15) and is very understandable in view of the Preacher's conviction that all is vanity. It is not as if God has turned his back on the world; he may be inaccessible and remote, but he definitely intervenes in what happens between people on earth.

In 8:10-15 we found that the Preacher denies all retribution by God. In verse 2 it seems he wants to emphasize this idea even more strongly, for here he is so unambiguous that there can be no mistaking his meaning. There is no difference in fate between the good and the evil; it does not matter whether a person is righteous or unrighteous, pure or impure; it makes no difference whether one is a participant in the offerings brought in the sanctuary or a nonparticipant; it is all the same whether one takes an oath or avoids taking an oath, as some people did at the time; in short, whether someone is a good person or a sinner has no effect. All without exception experience the same fate; this proves that there is no reward or retribution in accordance with moral standards. This is an absolutely revolutionary idea for the Old Testament. Here, in flat contradiction of the general view, the Preacher expressly states that the religious and moral qualities of man do not have the weight of a feather in affecting his fate. It is no wonder that later Judaism was shocked by the Preacher's position—he shakes the foundations of Judaism.

An interpretation now follows, as was the case in 8:11, that refers to the wickedness of man (v. 3). The Preacher finds it entirely normal that, in such circumstances, humanity is filled with wickedness and ignorance (the opposite of obedient wisdom). Why try so hard to do good if goodness makes no difference? But that is not yet the last word. If someone should claim that the essential difference in one's fate does not appear until after death, the Preacher answers in advance that that is not true, for at the end everyone meets the same destiny. Everyone goes the same way: to the dead. "The dead" is the collective term for all who have died and are together in the realm of the dead, and there is no distinction between those who have done well and those who have done evil in this life.

Suddenly, in verse 4, the Preacher strikes a different note: there is hope for those who live well. But beware; we know by this time that he loves to weave seemingly positive thoughts into a pessimistic passage, and do not doubt that he is about to do it now. In fact, in the next two lines he undertakes a sharp attack on the wisdom teachings of his day. First he cites a proverb: "A living dog is better than a dead lion." In form this is a "better than" proverb, which the wisdom teachers so much favored. In content it sings the praises of life over death. Even the despised animal (the dog) is better than the royal animal (the lion) when the first is alive and the second dead.

Has the Preacher forgotten what he said in 7:1-4 about the advantage of death over life? He answers this question in the next verse by giving his reason: the "advantage" of the living is that they know they must die while those who are already dead lack even this knowledge. Such bitter irony! The "advantage" is no advantage, and the Preacher by no means contradicts himself. He robs accepted wisdom of its power by using one of its typical genres, with a positive-sounding content and all, to voice his own bitter thoughts. By linking the thought of death so ironically to his conviction that there is no retribution he even accentuates the pronouncements he has made on the subject in the preceding chapter (8:14). Death, ironically, serves as "compensation" for all the injustice that takes place on earth. But if people cannot hope for justice after death they really have nothing to hope for.

The last part of the passage not only praises joy (cf. 8:15) but is a call to the enjoyment of life. It is also longer than the other joy passages we encountered so far (3:12-13, 22; 8:15)—which makes sense after the intense bitterness of the preceding words. His call comes in four parts. First of all, bread and wine should be enjoyed with a glad heart. In the ancient East these kinds of food were essential marks of a good life (cf. Ps. 104:14-15). If someone can answer this call it is a sign that God takes pleasure in his work (v. 7), for it is he who withholds or grants such things (cf. 2:25).

The second part of the appeal concerns the external signs of joy. White clothing is such a sign—that is why the custom arose among the Jews to wear white clothes on the sabbath (cf. Rev. 7:9). Oil is a desirable means of anointing, and may not be used in times of sorrow (see 2 Sam. 14:2).

In the third part the Preacher advises his reader to enjoy life with the wife he loves (v. 9). He therefore gives her a share in the enjoyment of life and does not just make her an object of pleasure. This is one of the reasons why it is unthinkable that the Preacher, in 7:26ff., should offer a fundamentally negative evaluation of women. General wisdom literature is familiar with a similar concept of enjoying the companionship of one's wife (e.g., Prov. 5:18-19), but here, as always, the function of the statement is unique. The rest of verse 9 reminds the reader of the toilsome vanity of life and that God is the giver of the occasions of enjoyment. It is typical for the author to keep bringing this up whenever joy crops up, for in this manner he continually reminds his readers that even the enjoyment of life is nothing positive. At best it is a substitute for despair; and in any case it is itself unpredictable, for God can at any moment withdraw the opportunity for it.

The fourth part of the call consists in saying that people should take advantage of the opportunities life offers them. This does not mean that human labor can be something meaningful after all but rather that it can sometimes be part of the enjoyment of life. That there is nothing truly positive in labor is evident from the second part of verse 10. It is relatively positive, however, but only because in the realm of the dead there is no more opportunity for labor or wisdom. But if that is the only reason for taking advantage of the opportunities of life there is no truly positive or permanent element in all the strivings of man. Labor is only a painkiller that helps a person forget the essential meaninglessness of life.

Summary

Thought:	Correct conduct
Counterthought:	Wrong conduct
Tension:	No retribution; everything ends in death

In the exposition of 8:10-15 we have dealt with the question how these thoughts relate to modern life. In addition we must also consider the question what the Preacher's view of the enjoyment of life and labor brings with it for Christian believers today. Joy on earth is certainly a good possibility for those who have been rescued from the dead-end road on which the Preacher finds himself. But the reason for joy now becomes totally different: joy no longer serves as a narcotic with which to kill the pain of a life without content or direction. The point is now to make grateful use of the opportunities God has given. On the other hand it does not change the meaning of human existence one bit if the life of a given believer has little or no opportunity for enjoyment or pleasure in it. For one's destiny is no longer the abode of the dead but the breakthrough of the kingdom of God in Christ. For that reason the last word on joy cannot be spoken before the arrival of the banquet of the Lord (Matt. 26:29). The same thing applies to opportunities for labor. They cannot possibly serve only as a means of helping people forget the bitterness of their lot, for Christ has opened the perspective of service. Service to one's fellowmen—with the intent that they too can have joy in life—means faithfulness to him who gives us orders. And after that comes the final call to the enjoyment of life: "Well done, good and faithful servant; you have been faithful over a little, I will set you over much; enter into the joy of your master" (Matt. 25:21).

NOTHING DEPENDS ON MAN 9:11-12

This poem links up with the preceding one in the sense that here too there is the unexpected absence of appropriate consequences for certain deeds. In this instance the point is that human skill or ability is no guarantee of success. Two strophes of four lines each impart a symmetrical structure to the poem. The first one (v. 11) offers a report of an observation, introduced by the same formula ("I saw") that occurred in 4:1 and 4:7. The second strophe (v. 12) is the conclusion arising from the first.

The Preacher mentions five instances of human skill, three of which also refer to wise men (the wise, the intelligent, the men of skill). This indicates that he is opposing accepted wisdom and that the first two instances (swift athletes and brave soldiers) are intended only as specific illustrations of skill and wisdom. When the Preacher says that the race is not "to the swift" he does not mean that all races are won by less fleet-footed athletes. The swiftest athletes, however, cannot count on winning. Nor can strong soldiers simply count on success in battle, nor are wealth and popularity the necessary consequences of wisdom. The best athlete can incur an injury; the weaker army can win a battle, as in the case of Gideon and his battle against the superior Mideonites (Judg. 7); and wisdom can be robbed of success by a variety of circumstances as the Preacher will soon show in 10:9-11.

The Preacher refers to these unexpected events as "time and chance." That is clear proof that his notion of time (cf. 3:1-9, 17) refers not just to the ceaseless progression of hours and days but also to the things that come unexpectedly and apart from human control. Some German theologians employ the expression "befalling time" for this purpose. It means pre-

111

cisely the same thing as "chance" or "lot," which, for the author, falls under the exclusive control of God. In other words, success does not depend on skill or wisdom but on the unpredictable and whimsical apportionments of God.

Of this kind of "time" man knows nothing. His ignorance is like that of a fish or a bird that is caught. If fish had any notion of what was to "befall" them, they would not be caught in the net. If the birds had understood their fate, they would not have been caught in the birdcatcher's snare. So one may conclude that human beings are as ignorant as fish and birds, for they allow themselves to be trapped in "evil times." These misfortunes fall on people suddenly, so that they have no opportunity to free themselves. Not that everything that happens to people is an "evil time" or a misfortune, according to the Preacher. It is a fact that such misfortunes do "befall" people, but there is also a chance that they do not happen. So the Preacher says that misfortunes happen "at an evil time," which implies there are also other times. Sometimes the swift do win a race; sometimes the strong do win a battle; sometimes skill and wisdom do succeed—but the reverse may happen just as easily. Therefore everything is uncertain and unreliable.

Summary

Thought:	General wisdom
Counterthought:	God's doings (time and chance)
Tension:	Uncertainty and unreliability of wisdom

This passage offers us a good illustration of the implications of the great poem on time (3:1-9). If there is a time for everything, favorable and unfavorable things simply happen haphazardly. Therefore wisdom, too, is subject to caprice. This time its relative value lies not in that it is stronger than folly (as in 1:12ff. and other places) but in that chance sometimes allows it to succeed. But this very fact only highlights how powerless human skill is, for ultimately everything depends on the unfathomable operations of a higher power.

It is not impossible that Paul in Romans 9:16 is making an allusion to Ecclesiastes 9:11. He says that nothing depends upon man's will or exertion, but all depends on God, who is merciful. Both this idea and the image of a runner correspond to this poem in Ecclesiastes. Nevertheless, Paul's concept is very different from that of the Preacher. Paul adds, after all, that the God on whom everything depends has mercy on mankind; this enables him to put his trust in God. By contrast there is not a trace of compassion in the God of the Preacher's view; consequently, the frustration of uncertainty in the face of a superior power makes it impossible for him to seek refuge in God.

We must not attempt to change this state of affairs, reading the Preacher as though he were Paul. The conceptual world of the Preacher is totally different from the world of faith that is Paul's, even aside from the question whether Paul in Romans 9 is in fact alluding to Ecclesiastes 9. And this could hardly be otherwise: the Preacher has not met the Christ who changed the entire outlook and life of the New Testament apostle (see Acts 9).

WISDOM AND SOCIAL DISCRIMINATION 9:13–10:1

As he has repeatedly done before, the Preacher divides his poem into two strophes, the first one giving his observation and the second his conclusion. In this instance both parts (9:13-15 and 9:16–10:1) consist of seven lines. The first strophe tells a short story whose purpose is to teach, and the second contains four proverbs that comment on the story.

The formula with which the passage opens ("I also saw . . .") indicates by the word *also* there there is a connection between this observation and the preceding (vv. 11-12). The Preacher adds that he was "greatly impressed" (NIV) by an example of wisdom, showing how important shrewd observation was to him. This again shows that he does indeed pay much attention to the subject of wisdom.

The actual story is told in verses 14 and 15. They tell of a city under siege. There is a sharp contrast between the two parties at war: the city is small and the attacking king is powerful. As is evident from the large-scale engineering equipment the attacker brings to the project, the city-dwellers do not have a chance against him. But wait—help may come from another direction. There is in the city a wise man able to

113

devise a plan for ending the siege—the weak have to be wily. Twice, however (thus with emphasis), the wise man is said to be poor as well. And there lies the problem—no one pays attention to him and therefore his wisdom does no one any good.* His poverty casts up a barrier between him and his fellow city-dwellers. This means that by a social prejudice based on class consciousness wisdom is made nonoperational with the result that the city is not saved.

The focal point of the story comes to immediate expression in the "better than" proverb of verse 16. That is the first of the four pronouncements that constitute the Preacher's conclusion. The advantage of wisdom over strength is well attested in general wisdom circles (see Prov. 21:22; also 20:18; 24:5-6), but the Preacher stresses the unfortunate side of the story. Only half a line is given to the advantage of wisdom, but a full line, embracing two parallel pronouncements, is devoted to the disadvantages: the impoverished wise man has to endure contempt, and no one listens to him. This is a phenomenon that occurs all too often, namely, that people judge the value of statements not by their content and quality, but by the standing the speaker has in the community.

Verse 17 is a repetition of the positive element. Although the reference is not specifically to a military situation (it is general and concerns only the wise and the foolish), it is clear from the context that the Preacher contrasts the quiet deliberations of the wise with the shouting of a commander of unthinking soldiers. Both the "more than" proverbial form and the thought itself are characteristic of established wisdom, but their function is to undermine the self-confidence of wise men. This is evident from the mocking words that bring out vividly the irony implied in the seemingly optimistic proverb. Just a moment ago, in verse 16, a positive rule was negated by a negative one; now the same thing happens in verse 18.

It is true that wisdom is better than weapons of war, for the poor wise man had the means, and suggested the possibility, of rescuing the little city from the power of the great king. This is the third "better than" proverb in this poem that

---

*Note that the author's translation of 9:15 differs from RSV, NIV, etc. It reads as follows: "And there was found in it [the city] a poor (but) wise man; he could have saved the city by his wisdom, but no one thought about that poor man."—Trans.

could just as well have been a part of Proverbs. But again its content is torpedoed by the Preacher—this time with more force and finality than in verse 16. This is clearer from the Hebrew text than from the English translation, in which there are different-sounding words for "better than" and "much good." In Hebrew, however, these words sound similar so that the author can produce a play on them. He says that by means of one transgression (not "sinner" as in RSV and NIV, a translation due to a scribal error) "a lot of good" (TEV) can be undone. However many "better than" proverbs are invented, the effect of one mistake is so strong that it can put that which is good out of business. For that reason the wisdom repeatedly said to be "good" really means nothing. This was clear from the story of the first strophe, where the single error not to consult the wise man brought with it the downfall of the city.

This idea is confirmed in the last two lines, which shows that 10:1 really belongs at the end of chapter 9. The ointment of the perfumer is very good, but one or two dead flies can spoil the entire supply. This is also the case with folly: a tiny bit of it is enough to have a bigger impact than wisdom— even with honor added. This provides a fine illustration of the Preacher's love for working out, with increasing intensity, a thought once stated. For him wisdom is obviously better than folly, but folly can destroy wisdom; even a small pinch of folly can do the job.

Summary

Thought:	Wisdom
Counterthought:	Folly
Tension:	Relative advantage of wisdom

But

Thought:	Wisdom
Counterthought:	The vagaries of destiny (discrimination)
Tension:	Worthlessness of wisdom

The concern of this poem is not with things that really happened. Although the Preacher possibly knew of an occurrence that occasioned the example of the poor wise man, the story remains just that: a story that aims to teach. This aim is to offer a comparative evaluation of wisdom while at the same time making clear its ultimate futility; it is not to polemicize against social discrimination. The element of class distinction is not an isolated component in the passage but serves to illumine the real subject from another angle—something that has happened repeatedly in the book. By this technique the Preacher builds up his argument in favor of his general pessimism. Already he has discussed wisdom in its connection with popular favor, corruption, possessions, sexual looseness, athletics, and personal misfortune, and the basic conclusion has been the same each time. If now the negative effect of class discrimination is added, it would seem that there is no area of life left in which he could be refuted.

The Preacher truly cannot be refuted. There is no area of life in which human abilities and possibilities cannot be frustrated by other factors. We can only be deeply impressed with the honesty of this thinker. But although he knew precisely how to diagnose the evils of human life, he still had no notion of a cure. The physician had not yet come.

WISDOM AND SOCIAL CHAOS 10:2-7

The structure of this poem is symmetrical. Two strophes of three lines each enclose a centerpiece of two lines. The couplet in the center is again a parenthesis, like the ones we found in 7:19 and 8:12b-13. Apart from the inner cohesion of the poem itself, the passage links up with both the preceding and the following poems, since the themes of all three are related.

The first strophe begins by praising wisdom and criticizing folly. For the Hebrews the heart was the seat of intelligence and reflection, not of feeling, as it is with us. "The right" meant good fortune; "the left," bad fortune. Verse 2 then has nothing to do with political orientations but simply posits the thesis that the mind of the wise man steers him in the direction of good fortune while the reverse is true for the fool. This is the typical view of the wisdom teachers, namely, that they are able to produce happiness in life.

The next two lines (v. 3) illustrate this point by accentuating the wretched consequences of folly. Even though the fool merely goes out on the street, he already experiences all the consequences of his lack of intelligence. There is no attempt to describe his errors here, but the effect is clearly stated: he shows everyone how stupid he is. His public behavior is so foolish that it is noticed all around (cf. Prov. 17:28). Wisdom, therefore, is greatly to be preferred over folly.

But the second strophe reverses the train of thought again. The very formula in which the Preacher announces that he has observed something contains the negative judgment that it concerns an evil matter. It concerns an error for which the ruler himself is responsible. Just as was done in the first strophe, so in the second the author uses the next two lines to put content into the statement. Verses 6 and 7 show that social chaos can arise as a result of action taken by the possessor of political power. The lowest social class is raised up and the highest class is humiliated. This reversal of the usual relationships is imitated by an ingenious arrangement of the words—something that cannot be conveyed in translation. The poetic rhythm in the Hebrew is a pattern of sound, so that 6a is long, 6b is short, 7a is short, and 7b is long. Poetically, then, verse 7 is the reverse of verse 6, a pattern that reflects the social reversal of which the two verses speak.

Ancient Eastern despots were able to bring about such revolutions with relative ease. Although the Preacher himself is not involved in action opposing such things, he does describe such a situation as wrong, that is, as something not in keeping with the social standards of the time. Then what use is wisdom if fools can have what really belongs to the wise? That is the point at issue here—not the relationship between the privileged class and the slave class. When social chaos comes as a result of the action of a despot, wisdom is helpless—no matter what accepted wisdom teaches on this point (cf. Prov. 16:14).

Central in the passage is verse 4. It offers the kind of advice wisdom teachers loved to give their disciples. The fickle temperament of a king is a threat to his surroundings (cf. Prov. 16:15). For that reason anyone in the presence of an angry ruler has to act circumspectly and remain calm to avoid taking a misstep. This is how the Preacher cites the characteristic optimism of his colleagues, at the same time surrounding it with his own pessimism, so that the result again becomes an attack on mainstream wisdom.

Summary

Thought:	Wisdom
Counterthought:	Folly
Tension:	Relative advantage of wisdom

And

Thought:	Wisdom
Counterthought:	Vagaries of destiny (social chaos)
Tension:	Worthlessness of wisdom

As in the preceding poem, so here the social sphere is the arena in which man's inability to intervene in life may be observed. But here the Preacher deals with another aspect of it, namely, social chaos. Yet he does not issue a call for (our notion of) justice. In fact, he utters no protest against a situation in which an arbitrary ruler elevates folly over wisdom, yet neither does he approve of granting status to slaves at the expense of the socially respectable. Of course, Christian reflection on the structures of society is timely and necessary, but it is not something to be learned from the Preacher. All he has accomplished is to show, once again, how untrustworthy the mental capacities of human beings are.

FRUSTRATION ON THE JOB 10:8-11

Again we have a poem whose structure is symmetrical. Verses 8a and 9a both begin with verbs having to do with "digging," and 8b and 9b begin with verbs having to do with "breaking." Similarly, verses 10 and 11 belong together: both are composed of a conditional (10a and 11a) and a consequence (10b and 11b). This is the final comment of the Preacher on the subject of the worthlessness of wisdom.

If someone were to work on a boundary wall in a field, a snake might bite him (8b). Not that it is certain, but the possibility exists. The work of a farmer is vulnerable to a chance element on which his skill has no effect. If this is a correct reading of the text, then the first half of the verse must also have to do with some aspect of agriculture or industry because the two halves of the verse run parallel (as in v. 9). So we conclude that verse 8a does not deal with the construction of a trap or an ambush (cf. Prov. 26:27; 28:10). Anyone whose work has to do with the digging of holes may have an accident on which he could not exert any influence. The same possibility is twice repeated in verse 9. Digging holes, working at stone walls around fields, demolition work, carpentry— they are all instances of human labor. Now then, says the Preacher, each of these instances shows that human skill and craftsmanship are always attended by dangers and possible frustrations, because outside elements over which we have no control can injure us, making the work worthless.

Verse 10 is an extremely difficult verse because in the process of being copied over, the Hebrew letters have been disarranged. Fortunately we can determine its meaning with the aid of verse 11 because the two verses are parallel. Verse 11 cites the example of the snake charmer, whose professional skill keeps the snake under control. It may also happen, however, that the snake bites before it can be charmed into submission. In that case all the charmer's skill cannot profit him. The preceding verse should express the same idea but with a different example, that of an ax. If the ax is dull and the cutting edge is not sharpened, then the woodsman who uses it has to apply more force: the tool demands more effort. The question then follows: What advantage is there in wisdom under these circumstances?* The assumed answer to this rhetorical question is clearly that wisdom is absolutely meaningless. The ax (v. 10) corresponds to the snake (v. 11), and wisdom is in a parallel position to the art of snake charming. The argument then runs like this: If an instrument is dull (the ax), it causes trouble that cannot be helped by wisdom, just as an "object" on which wisdom is supposed to have influence (the snake) can put wisdom out of action.

Basic to all the examples referred to in this paragraph is the same idea. This is already suggested by the tight unity of the poem: it ends as it began by speaking of a snake. At first glance we might think that the Preacher is offering useful advice, communicated to his disciples by way of real-life illustrations. He could be interpreted as saying that people should be careful when undertaking to do manual labor. But

*The author translates the last line of v. 10: ". . . is wisdom profitable or successful?" See J. A. Loader, *Polar Structures in the Book of Qohelet*, p. 63; see his discussion of this entire verse on pp. 64-65.—Trans.

the examples can be interpreted equally well as a denial of the possibility that one can prevent accidents—injuries and accidents simply happen.

So what we have here in fact is the Preacher's typical two-sidedness. On the one hand, his words sound like the conventional wisdom of the book of Proverbs; on the other, their content is charged with precisely the opposite meaning. So it is a case of general wisdom and its advice versus the author's pessimism. This is how the Preacher carries on his unceasing polemic against established wisdom.

Summary

Thought:	Wisdom
Counterthought:	Uncertain eventualities
Tension:	Worthlessness of wisdom resulting from this uncertainty

Although there are still more poems ahead of us in Ecclesiastes, this is the last in which the Preacher launches his attack specifically against all conventional wisdom. The principal characteristic of this offensive is that the author robs wisdom of its certainty (cf. 1:12–2:26; 4:13-16; 7:5-7; 7:11-14; 7:15-22; 7:23–8:1; 8:16-17; 9:11-12; 9:13–10:1; 10:2-7). Again and again he demonstrates how tenuous is the claim of wisdom to being knowledge of the art of living—no person has life in his control, and since to have it in one's control is precisely the object of wisdom, wisdom is meaningless.

A Christian will definitely have to differ with the Preacher at this point but not before conceding that his attack on human certainty is decidedly wholesome. The kind of certainty to which ancient Eastern wisdom had come was a form of self-assurance that led to fossilization. The wisdom teachers of the time had built up a system that stored up all the answers ready-made but forgot the questions. Such certainty provides a false sense of security; and one can only agree that under these conditions self-doubt is wholesome. But if that were the last word, the demolition process would have left only a vacuum. It is here that the difference in perspective lies between us and the Preacher. For we are in a position to know that this vacuum has been filled by Christ. By faith we may have assurance of this. Yet this faith does not mean we have to lapse into a system of false security; it does not imply that we have all the answers and that we never wrestle with the problems of life. Anyone who confuses the assurance of faith with self-sufficiency has failed to grasp the essence of the Christian faith. For such a person there is no better medicine than Ecclesiastes.

THE WORDS OF THE IGNORANT 10:12-15a

At the beginning of this poem we are again informed of the advantage wisdom has over folly, but here the specific context is that of human speech. Wise words are being praised while foolish talk is considered the cause of a person's downfall. As is his habit, the Preacher stresses the negative: in the remainder of the poem he concentrates on foolish talk.

The two halves of verse 13 show that such words create havoc—and that without exception. This is indicated by the two opposites "beginning" and "end," which in Hebrew together describe a totality and so refer to all the words of the fool.

Verses 14a and 15a are closely akin, and between them we again find a parenthesis—one of the author's favorite devices (see also 7:19; 8:12b-13; 10:4). He is not so much positing a thesis here as heaving a sigh. As a rule fools have much to say, but when do they ever get tired of talking so that the chatter stops? So, superficially, the Preacher means simply that silence is better than foolish words. That is one of the most common themes of conventional wisdom literature (cf. Prov. 10:11; 12:14; 13:3; 15:2; etc.). But when we scrutinize the matter more closely we notice that the parenthesis, inserted in verse 14b, introduces a totally new point of view. Twice we read how ignorant a human being really is. In the first statement this is simply asserted; in the second the point is made by a rhetorical question with the same content. Unless we assume that the parenthesis landed here by mistake and should not really be taken seriously, this combination of ideas means that much talk is harmful in view of man's ignorance. Although speech is not prohibited, and wise words are even applauded, it turns out that all human beings are ignorant of what life holds for them and that silence is therefore better than speech. For to speak of matters of which one is ignorant spells trouble.

Summary

Thought:	Permissible speech
Counterthought:	Preferable silence
Tension:	Ignorance about the eventualities of life

In the teaching of established wisdom teachers the entire topic of speech and silence is treated with optimistic advice to their disciples. That is precisely the way they seek to clear up areas of ignorance and foster knowledge of the art of living. In their opinion, by speaking and by refraining from speech at the right time, a person can exert influence over the course of his or her life. The Preacher, however, turns this around. According to him, man's point of departure is ignorance, and the result is that he can by no means say he has life in his control. So in essence he is here giving us a summary of his lengthy treatment of the subject of speech in 5:1-9, where a variety of cult-related and social aspects of the issue came up.

SILENCE IS BETTER THAN PROTEST 10:15b-20*

The way verse 15 reads in most translations it makes no sense. It is hard to conceive how the reason for the exhaustion of the fool can consist in that he does not know his way to the city (see KJV), especially because the reason is already assumed when it is said that his labor wearies him (toilsome labor wears him out). Besides, in the Hebrew text of verse 15 there are many difficulties in gender and number that indicate that confusion has arisen in the copying process. There is a simple solution to the problem, however; it is that the last part of

---

*The author here inserts verse 15b within verse 16 and translates it differently from the standard English versions to give the following translation:

16a Woe to you, O Land, whose king is a child
15b who does not know enough to consult a counselor
16b and whose princes feast in the morning.

—Trans.

verse 15 and the first part of verse 16 have been transposed by mistake. When these two are reversed back to the original order a meaningful conclusion to the previous poem (12-15a) emerges, as well as a precise parallelism between the woe-cry and the beatitude with which the new poem (vv. 16[+15b]-20) opens.

Thus the first two lines of the poem consist of three parts each and concern the king of a land, the princes of that kingdom, and an added element. The Preacher considers unfortunate a country whose king is a mere stripling who has no appreciation for the advice of a counselor. The rare Hebrew word for "counselor" used here has the same sound as the common word for "city," which explains how the misunderstanding relating to "the way to the city" crept in.* Similarly, it is a disaster for a country when its princes start partying in the morning, that is, when they get drunk and act irresponsibly. Something like that happened in the time of Rehoboam when he accepted the advice of irresponsible young contemporaries in preference to the wise words of older counselors (1 Kings 12:6ff.). Appreciation for the advice of counselors is also a familiar subject in wisdom literature (see Prov. 11:14; 13:10; 19:20; 20:18). Verse 17 makes the opposite statement that a land is blessed whose king is of noble birth and therefore does what he is supposed to, and whose princes dine at the proper time and thus act responsibly.

Verses 18 and 19 at first do not seem to be related to these ideas, but they are actually closely connected. First the Preacher, in his well-known way, cites a proverb from the treasury of conventional wisdom (v. 18). He expresses criticism of laziness—a criticism that appears often in the book of Proverbs (e.g., Prov. 19:15, 24; 24:30ff.; 26:13, 16). Laziness is a vice that causes injury. If we now turn to verse 19 we notice that it offers a description of the wretched conditions in which the woe-cry was raised. The unsound people who cause injury to the state are interested only in the pleasures of feasting and wine; they form the elite around the king who fails to do his duty. The final pronouncement of verse 19 ("money is the answer for everything") is probably a reference to corruption in the affairs of the state. The Preacher thereby

*See J. A. Loader, *Polar Structures in the Book of Qohelet*, footnote, p. 79.— Trans.

emphasizes the unfortunate situation of the woe-cry, and indicates that the content of the beatitude only serves as a foil to show how things ought to be.

The climax finally comes in the last two lines (v. 20): a double warning not to curse the notables of the land and the reason for it. Even an inaudible curse against the king should be avoided; the same goes for a curse against the rich uttered in the most private part of one's house. The king and the rich people here have to be those we heard about in the woe-cry of verse 16: the immature king and his irresponsible circle of high-society friends. Such potentates can cause discontent and frustration among the people, as the case of Rehoboam and his youthful advisors illustrates (1 Kings 12). It makes complete sense that an oppressed and exploited people will curse the prospering upper crust in their hearts and that they will want to vent their hostility in an inner room. But the Preacher advises against it and gives the reason that an unexpected and unforeseen element may enter the picture that would make the thoughts of the heart and the words of the bedroom known to the people in power and bring harm to the speakers. The author does not say how that might happen—which fits the point he wants to make, namely, that the unthinkable can happen. He does illustrate the point, though: the birds may hear and report the words. (This is a very different sentiment from that of the South African poet Louis Leipoldt who believes that "one thing is certain: / the birds will never tell!") The unforeseeable element, which crops up so frequently in Ecclesiastes, is here represented by the birds. They have the same function as the eventualities of life or destinies that come over people according to other poems in the book.

To people who are unhappy with the conduct of those in power the Preacher's advice is that they should be silent—even though he knows that those in power have done wrong (v. 16).

Summary

Thought:	Speech (cursing)
Counterthought:	The unexpected element
Tension:	Danger to the speaker

At this point we have perhaps the most graphic illustration of the difference between the Preacher and the great prophets of Israel. The prophets could not be silent, being fired up by God to speak (e.g., Ezek. 3:16ff.) and to protest against the injustice that people in power commit (e.g., Isa. 5:8ff., where one finds remarkable similarities with the depiction in this poem, and Jer. 20:7ff., where we see how the prophet sometimes wanted to be silent but was not permitted by God). Just as in 4:1-3, where the author shows that he has no comfort to offer the oppressed, he makes it very plain here that for them there is no relief. By linking the idea of corruption and injustice with the subject of speech and silence, he indicates that protest, far from being valuable, is dangerous.

It is evident by now that the elements the Preacher adopts from general wisdom again function in a way opposite to their original role in the literature of the wisdom teachers and that they must therefore be read as criticism of these teachers.

The Preacher remains in the dead-end street—for him there is no relief. In essence, however, it is the dead-end street on which all people find themselves. He attests indirectly, then, that another way of escape, from another direction, needs to be opened up to human beings. The one who finds this way of escape will not be able to keep quiet about it—much less than the Preacher, who, though conscious of the danger of speech, nevertheless gave us his words, words that continue to fascinate us to this very day.

RISK AND ASSURANCE 11:1-6

This next-to-the-last poem of the book has been carefully structured. The second half (vv. 4-6) consists of two parts (vv. 4-5 on the one hand, v. 6 on the other), each of which comprises a line concerning agricultural practice and two lines concerning human ignorance. This shows they are closely linked and have the same function; and that function is to illumine the theme of verses 1-3.

Verse 1 is one of the (few) familiar parts of the book. But, just as in the case of 3:1-9, familiarity is no guarantee of understanding. The RSV translates the verse: "Cast your bread upon the waters, for you will find it after many days."*

This translation, notwithstanding the renowned interpreters of the synagogue, the early church, and the Reformation who read the verse that way, is definitely incorrect. The Hebrew verb used here has an intensive (emphatic) meaning: it does not just mean "cast" or "throw" but "throw forth," "dispatch." Furthermore, the second half of the verse does not offer the reason for the first ("for"), but offers a counterthought that produces astonishment ("yet"). Moreover, in the context of the entire book and in particular in that of verses 4 and 5, it is inconceivable that the Preacher would suddenly summon his readers to do a noble deed (what would it consist of?) for which compensation would follow (and what kind of reward is it when people get back without interest what they have lost?). No one can find it convincing when he is told that the reason he should throw out his bread is simply that he may get it back again.

"Bread" can mean "possessions" (cf. 9:11, where bread parallels riches). Then the verse means that one can blithely "throw forth" one's possessions into the sea and nonetheless find them all back again. That, then, has to be taken as a reference to maritime trade, in which people can take incredibly bold risks and still not suffer loss.

This interpretation is confirmed by verse 2. Here we encounter the precise opposite. Divide your "bread" (i.e., your possessions) into seven or even eight parts in order, in the most responsible way possible, to avoid risk. This is what Jacob did when he was afraid that misfortune would befall the people and the possessions in his caravan, and this is how people still act today as they divide and diversify their investments to protect themselves from risk. But the Preacher adds that disaster may strike nevertheless, reducing this eightfold protective measure to nothing. Where loss is expected (in a situation where risky ventures are begun, v. 1), it may happen that not a penny is lost; and where no loss is

---

*But see the Good News Bible: "Invest your money in foreign trade, and one of these days you will make a profit. Put your investments in several places—many places even—because you never know what kind of bad luck you are going to have in this world." And compare the author's own translation: "Dispatch your bread across the water—yet, after many days, you may possibly find it again."—Trans.

expected (in a situation where an entire shipload is divided into a great many parts, v. 2) a complete catastrophe may ensue. If we now take a careful look at the order of these pronouncements in these two verses, we shall notice that they are related to each other in an X-pattern:

In 1a (incredible risktaking) we expect the result of 2b (loss); and in 2a (responsibility) we expect the result expressed in 1b (success)—but the reverse *may* happen. In other words, whatever one's choice of conduct may be, the outcome depends not on man himself but on a power over which he has no control. There is no way that risk can be eliminated, and consequently there is no certainty for man on earth.

Verse 3 stresses that things, being determined in advance, are not affected by human influence: if the clouds are heavy with water, it rains (and not in other circumstances); if a tree has to fall to the south, to the south it falls, and if it has to fall to the north, it falls only in that direction. In these proverblike statements there again lurks an assault on the essence of the wisdom of the ancient East. Whereas that wisdom was oriented to prosperity and success by teaching people how they could keep their grip on life, the Preacher maintains that there is no way one can influence one's own fate and that there can therefore be no assurance of success.

This ode to uncertainty could not be clearer. Still, the Preacher explains his viewpoint further with the use of examples from the sphere of agriculture (while verses 1 and 2 relate to the world of commerce). On first reading, verse 4 seems to be an ordinary proverb that gives expression to the thought that the farmer had better work rather than watch the weather. And indeed, if one views the proverb apart from the context, it is possible to read it that way. But this positive interpretation, which would be characteristic for wisdom in general, is negated by the remainder of the poem. The rain either comes or it does not come; it is not something man can do anything about—and he does not even know anything about it, for it lies within the domain of God's works. It is therefore useless to try to "read" the wind or the clouds to see if the rain will come. This negative idea may just as well be the import of the proverb, and the following two lines in fact indicate that this is the Preacher's intent. He says that man knows just as little of the work of God as he does of the way the spirit of life originates in an unborn child. There is an interesting wordplay in the text here, which is often overlooked by translators and commentators. In Hebrew the word for "wind" is the same as the word for "spirit," which helps us to understand why the Preacher should use the image of the spirit of an unborn child to clarify his pronouncements on the weather. God rules all things—regardless of man's field of vision and the human sphere of influence. Humans are then helpless beings who cannot count on security.

Verse 6 has the same function. This time the form of instruction is an admonition, of which there are numerous examples in general wisdom literature. The content is also so characteristic of the genre that the first line might just as well have been a text in Proverbs. It can easily be read as an exhortation to be industrious (cf. Prov. 6:6-11; 10:4-5; 20:4; 24:30ff.), but again the following lines make plain that that cannot be the author's intent: rather, work early and late because you do not know whether your morning work or your evening work will turn the tide in your favor or whether perhaps both will do well for you. This means that there is no connection whatever between the quality of the work done and its result; the outcome is determined by another power— not mentioned by name here, but one that has to be God (see v. 5). Again it is plain that the farmer has no certainty and his fortunes may turn out to his advantage or disadvantage.

Summary

Thought:	Risk
Counterthought:	Elimination of risk
Tension:	No security

But this poem also has to do with human knowledge and planning:

Thought:	Human "knowledge" and human action
Counterthought:	Life's eventualities
Tension:	No security

The contrast between the Preacher's enormous lack of security and the certainty of the New Testament is too striking to be ignored. The certainty exhibited by Paul, for instance, is rooted in his conviction that the disasters of life have no influence on the glorious outcome of all things since nothing can separate the believer from the love of God (Rom. 8:31-39). Because in Ecclesiastes there is no reference to the love of God but instead only to a huge chasm between God and man, it is no wonder there is no sense of security in the book. The Preacher shows the Christian how utterly uncertain all things would have been had God not intervened in his Son.

It would be wrong, however, to read Ecclesiastes solely from a New Testament perspective and with a pious sense of superiority. The skepticism the Preacher expresses toward cocky self-assurance also contains a wholesome element. The assurance of faith that naturally predominates in the New Testament does not mean that we as believers can move through life with complete self-assurance and with the favorable outcome of every undertaking always in sight. It is part of human responsibility to accept the challenge of new and distant horizons as we search for answers to the many questions and problems that confront and afflict us in numerous areas. The New World would never have been discovered if seafarers had been unwilling to let the European coastline disappear from their field of vision. The same thing applies to the world of thought and scholarship. If no one had ever been prepared to cut himself loose from familiar territory and to venture into the unknown, the great discoveries and breakthroughs from which we all now profit would never have taken place.

THEREFORE ENJOY YOURSELF! 11:7–12:8

In many respects this concluding poem is the most striking in the entire book. It consists of two parts: three times the first part issues a summons to go and enjoy life, each time followed by a negative element that puts a damper on the positive (11:7-10); and the second part contains the well-known imperative of 12:1a, followed by three groups of pronouncements on the degeneration occurring in old age (12:1b-2, 3-5, 6-7). That both the idea of enjoying life and that of the degeneration of life occur in threefold repetitions means that the Preacher intends to put a heavy emphasis on both. This is not surprising, for destruction and enjoyment are in a sense the two poles around which his thoughts turn. The poem thus constitutes an appropriate closing statement to the entire book because it summarizes the author's convictions.

In all other instances where his conclusion was expressed (3:12-13, 22; 8:15; 9:7-10), we could see how his negative conviction issued into his enjoy-yourself-if-you-can conclusion. Here, however, these two themes occur in reverse order: that which logically should have come first now comes last. This is very striking and indicates that the poem was specially composed to serve as the book's finale. By ending with the dark notes of death the Preacher shows that for him the negative tone of the book is intentionally dominant. For that reason the book's first word and its last are identical, and the closing formula (v. 8) is the same as the opening formula (1:2): Vanity!

The poem starts at 11:7 with the optimistic idea of how pleasant life can be. Light is a symbol of life (cf. 7:1 on the lamp of life). Then the Preacher says what a person ought to do (v. 8): if he lives many years (there is a possibility, but no certainty, of this), he should enjoy himself; but he should also bear in mind the darkness of death, since it is sure to come and last a long time. The entire future is meaningless. This is how the Preacher introduces tension into the enjoyment theme.

Twice he sharpens up these themes. In verse 9 his tone becomes more personal because he stops speaking of "a man" in the abstract and turns directly to his students. This is the only indication in the entire book that he is addressing young men. As long as a person is young, he has to make the most of pleasure and enjoyment. Then comes the restrictive element: God brings everyone into judgment. That the Preacher means the judgment of death is indicated not only by the immediate context but also by his usual manner of speaking (see 8:6, where the same Hebrew word occurs, and also 3:17 and 8:11). Because this dark undertone recurs whenever the note of enjoyment is struck, we cannot share the opinion of those exegetes who want to delete the last line of this verse as a "pious addition." The same thing applies to the second accentuation of the negative aspect in verse 10, where the Preacher again sounds a somber note along with the call to enjoyment. Had composers ever wanted to set this poem to music, it might have been done best by Tchaikovsky, for he knew how to bring into one harmony both dark tones and sounds of joy.

In the second part of the poem (starting at 12:1), the young man is told to remember his Creator in his youth. Some interpreters find even this admonition too pious for the Preacher and so they want to amend it. This is not acceptable, for God is the giver of the eventualities of life and the admonition is consistent with the way the Preacher has used the idea of creation in 3:11. The pleasures of which we heard in the previous part end with the only certainty there is for the Preacher—death. Death is just as much at God's disposal as occasions for pleasure and all the other things in life. So the admonition of 12:1a changes, without a break, into a moving description of human frailty.

Burdensome and unpleasant days are ahead (v. 1b); the light of life, mentioned in 11:7-8, grows dim and is clouded over (v. 2). Verses 3 and 4 are an allegory: an entire household serves as a picture of the human body. The "keepers of the house," that is, the arms, begin to tremble; the "strong men," the legs, are bent (for the opposite image, see Song of Sol. 5:15); the "grinders" are the teeth, which, because they are so few in number, have stopped working and therefore can no longer make food fit to be swallowed; "those that look through the windows," the eyes, are dim; and the "doors on the street," the ears, are shut so that the everyday sounds of the house are not audible anymore—the voices of the aged tend to become high in tone and low in volume. Verse 5 continues the same train of thought with a new set of images. Old people develop a variety of fears: outside, spring has come and nature springs alive, but the aged do not appreciate it anymore. The contrast here is striking: blossoms appear in the trees and insects have food in abundance (that is what 5b means, not that the grasshopper "drags itself along," as in RSV, NIV, TEV), but precisely the opposite process is at work in the greybeard. The body's household is in a state of collapse and man is on his way to his eternal home—the abode of the dead.

In verse 6 a new set of images begins, this time from the realm of living water (cf. John 4:10ff.). The cord, the bowl (or bucket), the jug, the wheel at the cistern—all the equipment for drawing and using fresh water—are broken, and death sets in. The reference to gold and silver equipment indicates that all these parts on which life itself depends are precious. There is nothing in verse 7 to hint or suggest that the spirit of a person goes to heaven and only the body perishes. This verse would then contradict the rhetorical question of 3:21, which asserts that the lifebreath (the same word as "spirit" in Hebrew) does *not* go upward. It would also clash with 3:20 (that man and animal both end up the same) and with the entire thrust of the poem, not to mention the rest of the book. Important here is only the idea that the principle of life is in God's hands. He gives life, he takes it back. Without that principle no human existence is possible.

The final statement can rightly conclude everything, then—it is all the height of futility! Everything ends in nothing!

Summary

Over and over in the book we saw one pole of thought in tension with another. Now we observe the outcome:

Pole A ——————— emptiness, tension ——————— Pole B

Make the most of an evil situation!

In the final poem the ideas of the degenerative process and of youthful enjoyment oppose each other. The negative note is stronger, however, making the value of life's enjoyments relative. These two opposing poles differ from all the ones we have seen heretofore in one respect though: one is a consequence of the other. So the case is this: the Preacher summons man to enjoy himself, not despite the futility of life but in consequence of that futility. This idea was a very prevalent one—for example, in Greek sources of roughly the same period as the Preacher. That does not make him a Greek in Hebrew clothing; he is too much an original thinker to be viewed as a common borrower. But others do borrow from him: the well-known student song "Gaudeamus igitur" ("Let us therefore rejoice as long as we are young") so strongly echoes parts of the poem that it was probably inspired by it.

The apostle Paul also views this kind of inference ("enjoy yourself") as a natural consequence of an empty life. If all things issue into the darkness of death, then we should "eat and drink, for tomorrow we die" (1 Cor. 15:32). But to Paul that outcome is only a theoretical possibility, mentioned as a foil in order to accentuate the positive Christian conviction that the last enemy of man has been overcome in principle (1 Cor. 15:12) and that its destruction will take place in the end (1 Cor. 15:26).

For everyone who believes that a destination other than Hades or Sheol awaits us, the Preacher's call takes on a different color. Capitalize on every opportunity for as long as it is available, he says. For Christians that will mean they must make the most of their time for the sake of other people (Col. 4:5). Be glad, says the Preacher. To this cry the Christian will assent—not, however, as a painkiller in the distress of life but because Christ has overcome the distressing causes of the distress of life (Phil. 4:4).

THE EPILOGUE 12:9-14

The epilogue is obviously not the work of the Preacher. It refers to him in the third person and the past tense (vv. 9-10), uses the typical form of address "my son" (v. 12), something the Preacher never does, and openly takes issue with him (vv. 12-14). This section contains a number of difficult expressions—something the reader can quickly learn by comparing the translations of various interpreters. It tends toward being poetry yet without being poetry.

Still, its meaning is generally clear. There are two parts, namely, verses 9-11, which are the work of a disciple of the Preacher, and verses 12-14, which are the work of a critic.

In verse 9 the writer expressly says that the words that follow are an added appendix; he writes as an admirer of the Preacher. In keeping with the practice of the time he provides at the end of the scroll some data concerning the author. He regards the Preacher as a sage and a teacher of the people, stressing his perspicacity and literary activity rather than his identity and origin. The Preacher composed many maxims and was as diligent about quantity as he was about quality. According to verse 10, his pronouncements had two chief characteristics: they were pleasing—that is, they flattered eye and ear and were very ingenious in form—and at the same time they were honest words of truth. No one who has read the book attentively will deny this. The Preacher is an astute artist and a master of form, balance, and words. But he is also an honest poet who does not just give the masses what they want to hear. His words clearly and undeniably express his own inner convictions, however disconsolate they may be.

It is therefore fitting that the redactor-disciple of the Preacher should in verse 11 add a proverb, as his master loved to do, and that in a style very typical of the master. The words of the wise are like goads, akin to those by which draft animals are driven or led. This is a reference to the element of pain there is in wisdom, something the Preacher himself was conscious of (7:5); yet it is wholesome even when it is not pleasant to listen to. This characterization applies to no book of wisdom more than to Ecclesiastes. The second figure of verse 11 is more difficult. Mention is made of nails, which clearly parallel the goads of the driver, but the last expression is uncertain. It is often translated as the "collected sayings" (RSV). Recently a commentator proposed that one should think rather of the main themes of the book. That is very well possible, for the reference is literally to "the heads of the collection"; and the "heads," being parallel with "words," cannot refer to people. Perhaps the nails, which when driven down fasten objects to each other, are the sharp quotations the Preacher keeps borrowing from general wisdom and around which he then builds his own ideas. Finally, the redactor-disciple stresses the trustworthiness of the words of his teacher. They are given by one Shepherd. Since God is pictured as a Shepherd in the Old Testament (e.g., Ps. 23), we must understand the word in that way here. The disciple is then saying that his teacher was led by God and that the teaching of this remarkable man is therefore a service rendered to God. And that, too, is decidedly true—the incisive words of the book show undeniably how intensely we need God and how little we can trust our own systems of thought. The disciple is right—the tougher the Preacher's words are, the more effective they can be as instruments of God.

This is not, however, how a second reader understood them. In verse 12 this reader says that he wants to add a second appendix. Here he shows himself to be a member of the party the Preacher took so thoroughly to task, namely, the teachers of the established schools of wisdom. The first sign of his identity is the form of address he uses: "my son" (as in Prov. 1:8, 10, 15, etc.). Admiration for the Preacher's literary industry (vv. 9-10) has given way here to its opposite. While the first redactor says that the Preacher has arranged many proverbs with great care, the second remarks that the making of many books is an activity without limit; whereas the first redactor points out that the Preacher has sought to discover much, the second says that much study is only a weariness of the flesh. So he warns the reader of the book against uncritical adoption of the Preacher's thoughts: "My son, beware. . . ."

Finally, he offers his own idea of the sum of the matter when all is said and done (vv. 13-14). Considering everything, he condenses it into one line, and that is the orthodox Jewish conviction that God must be feared and his commandments kept. That is the standard by which all human beings will be measured: Have they kept the law? Judgment comes; even the hidden deeds of men will be judged as being either good or bad. Here, then, we have the doctrine of retribution, which constituted the operating principle of the general wisdom of the day. In the period that followed, that teaching was developed into the fundamental guideline of the Jewish religion because it was linked with the keeping of the law. Anyone who keeps the commandments of God's law is rewarded, and anyone who does not keep them is punished.

It is precisely this notion that the Preacher opposed; thus this section cannot possibly be viewed as the sum of his thoughts. Indirectly the second redactor shows how deep an impact the Preacher has had on his contemporaries. He cannot bring any counterarguments to bear, so he simply serves up a repetition of the doctrine of retribution (this time in its Jewish, law-oriented form). This redactor also unintentionally served the cause of his opponent, for his words at the end of the scroll formed one of the factors that contributed to the book's acceptance and retention in the list of holy Scriptures.

When we read Ecclesiastes from the perspective of the first redactor, we have before us a different book than when we read it from the standpoint of the second redactor. We can indeed tell the difference between the second redactor and the Preacher; yet the second postscript declares that the essence of the book is, Fear God and obey the commandments. At least, that is how he reads the book whether he is forced to make the statement by the status the book has gained before his time or not. And that has its value for us. Although we may differ with the writer of the second ending—just as we may differ with the Preacher himself—we have to admit that his words establish a kind of balance. That balancing assertion consists in the fact that the Preacher's declaration of futility and his enjoy-yourself theme can never cancel one's responsibility to be obedient. And with that the Christian is in agreement. When we learn from the Preacher how great our human need is, Christ then comes to bring redemption, and that calls for still another word: obedient gratitude.